Caderno do Futuro
A evolução do caderno

LÍNGUA INGLESA

Book 2
ENSINO FUNDAMENTAL

3ª edição
São Paulo - 2013

IBEP

Coleção Caderno do Futuro
Língua Inglesa – Book 2
© IBEP, 2013

Diretor superintendente	Jorge Yunes
Gerente editorial	Célia de Assis
Editor	Angelo Gabriel Rozner
Assistente editorial	Fernanda dos Santos Silva
Revisão	Rachel Prochoroff
	Maria Inez de Souza
Coordenadora de arte	Karina Monteiro
Assistente de arte	Marilia Vilela
	Nane Carvalho
	Carla Almeida Freire
Coordenadora de iconografia	Maria do Céu Pires Passuello
Assistente de iconografia	Adriana Neves
	Wilson de Castilho
Ilustrações	José Luís Juhas
Produção gráfica	José Antônio Ferraz
Assistente de produção gráfica	Eliane M. M. Ferreira
Projeto gráfico	Departamento Arte Ibep
Capa	Departamento Arte Ibep
Editoração eletrônica	N-Publicações

CIP-BRASIL. CATALOGAÇÃO-NA-FONTE
SINDICATO NACIONAL DOS EDITORES DE LIVROS, RJ

K38i
3.ed.

Keller, Victoria
 Língua inglesa : book 2, (7º ano) / Victoria Keller, pseudônimo dos autores Antonio de Siqueira e Silva, Rafael Bertolin. - 3. ed. - São Paulo : IBEP, 2013.
 il. ; 28 cm   (Caderno do futuro)

 ISBN 978-85-342-3569-3 (aluno) - 978-85-342-3573-0 (mestre)

 1. Língua inglesa (Ensino fundamental) - Estudo e ensino. I. Título. II. Série.

12-8684.   CDD: 372.6521
                            CDU: 373.3.016=111

27.11.12   03.11.12   041073

3ª edição - São Paulo - 2013
Todos os direitos reservados.

IBEP

Av. Alexandre Mackenzie, 619 - Jaguaré
São Paulo - SP - 05322-000 - Brasil - Tel.: (11) 2799-7799
www.editoraibep.com.br editoras@ibep-nacional.com.br

CTP, Impressão e Acabamento IBEP Gráfica
40154

SUMÁRIO

CONTENTS

LESSON 1 – VERB TO BE	4
LESSON 2 – VERB TO BE – SHORT ANSWER	9
LESSON 3 – DEFINITE AND INDEFINITE ARTICLES	12
REVIEW	16
LESSON 4 – ORDINAL NUMBERS	18
LESSON 5 – VERB TO BE – PAST TENSE	25
LESSON 6 – THERE IS… – THERE WAS…	31
LESSON 7 – PREPOSITIONS – I	38
LESSON 8 – PREPOSITIONS – II	44
LESSON 9 – VERB CAN (VERBO PODER)	47
REVIEW	50
LESSON 10 – COULD, COULD NOT	56
LESSON 11 – SIMPLE PRESENT	60
LESSON 12 – PRESENT CONTINUOUS TENSE	65
REVIEW	74
LESSON 13 – FUTURE WITH GOING TO	78
LESSON 14 – INTERROGATIVE WORDS I	86
LESSON 15 – INTERROGATIVE WORDS II	93
LESSON 16 – POSSESSIVE ADJECTIVES	100
LESSON 17 – POSSESSIVE CASE	103
LESSON 18 – DO, DOES	109
LESSON 19 – DO NOT, DOES NOT	113
ADDITIONAL TEXTS	119
GENERAL VOCABULARY	129

SUBJECT

NAME

TEACHER

HOUR	MONDAY	TUESDAY	WEDNESDAY	THURSDAY	FRIDAY	SATURDAY	SUNDAY

TESTS AND WORKS

Lesson 1 – Verb to be (present tense) – contracted form

- Hello! Who are you?
- I'm Robert, and you, what's your name?
- My name is Carol. How are you, Robert?
- I'm fine, thanks.

CONTRACTED FORM
(Forma contraída, abreviada)

Nos diálogos, é comum a utilização da forma contraída. A forma contraída consiste na substituição da vogal inicial das formas verbais por um apóstrofo.

Verb to be – Present tense

Forma por extenso	Forma abreviada, comum na conversação	Forma negativa
I am	I'm	I'm not
You are	You're	You're not / You aren't
He is	He's	He's not / He isn't
She is	She's	She's not / She isn't
It is	It's	It's not / It isn't
We are	We're	We're not / We aren't
You are	You're	You're not / You aren't
They are	They're	They're not / They aren't

Observações:

a) Não se usa a forma contraída quando a frase (afirmativa) tiver apenas o pronome e o verbo:
   - Are you well? (Você está bem?)
   - Yes, **I am**. (Sim, eu estou.)

b) Na linguagem coloquial, pode-se usar a forma contraída do verbo com nomes-sujeitos:

   My name's Carol.
   (Meu nome é Carol.)

c) Usa-se também com as palavras **that, how, what, where, who** (aquele, como, qual, onde, quem):

   What's your name?
   (Qual é o seu nome?)

d) Forma negativa abreviada

   Observe as duas formas:

   She isn't well.

   She's not well.

   (Ela não está bem.)

1. Escreva na forma abreviada. Observe o exemplo.

It is expensive. **It's expensive.**

a) It is cheap.

b) I am strong.

c) She is my girlfriend.

d) He is not well.

e) We are teachers.

f) They are good workers.

g) What is his name?

h) Where is her bike?

i) That is fine!

j) How is your mother?

2. Reescreva as frases, empregando a outra forma abreviada. Observe o exemplo.

We're not perfect.
We aren't perfect.

a) They aren't at school.

b) She's not your friend.

c) It's not hot.

d) You're not well.

e) He isn't rich.

f) She's not a lazy girl.

g) Jane's not here.

h) The boy's not tired.

3. Dê respostas negativas curtas (**short answers**). Observe o exemplo.

Is she well today?
No, she isn't.

a) Is Susan a beautiful girl?

b) Is this car expensive?

c) Is Mark at home?

d) Is this orange sweet?

e) Are these beaches clean?

f) Is this film interesting?

g) Is this your dog?

h) Are your parents Chinese?

i) Are you tall?

j) Are you American?

k) Are you right?

4. Dê respostas negativas por extenso. Observe o exemplo.

Are you Brazilian?
No, I am not Brazilian.

a) Are they English?

b) Are you well?

c) Is it cold today?

d) Is it warm?

e) Are your parents angry?

f) Is Julie hungry?

g) Are you thirsty?

5. Responda de forma afirmativa ou negativa.

a) Is it an apple?

b) Is this a fruit?

c) Are these magazines?

c) It – near – far

d) She – strong – weak

d) Are those ships?

e) The model – fat – thin

f) They – American – Mexican

g) I – tall – short

6. Responda as questões seguindo o exemplo abaixo.

She – funny – serious
She's not funny.
She's serious.

h) The film – interesting – boring

a) I – teacher – dentist

b) I – John – William

7. Reescreva as frases na forma abreviada. Observe o exemplo.

It is an orange.
It's an orange.

a) Who is that boy?

b) Where is my key?

c) What is his name?

d) What is your name?

e) Where is she from?

f) You are right.

g) We are at home.

h) They are at school.

Dictation

9. Ouça com atenção o ditado que o professor vai apresentar e escreva.

Lesson 2 – Verb to be – short answer

> Is Jeff a good fisherman?
>
> Yes, he is.
>
> And Jane? Is she a good fisherwoman?
>
> No, she's not.

1. Traduza o diálogo acima.

2. Dê respostas curtas. Observe o exemplo.

Are Jeff and Jane at school?
No, they are not.

a) Are Jeff and Jane fishing?

b) Is the Amazon river long?

c) Is sugar sour?

d) Are Brazilian beaches beautiful?

e) Are Brazilian football players famous?

f) Is honey sweet?

g) Is lemon sweet?

h) Is China a very populous country?

i) Are young models thin?

e) young – old
— Are your grandparents young?

3. Observe o exemplo e responda às perguntas.

short – tall
— Are you short?
— No, I am not.
I am tall.

f) near – far
— Is your school near?

a) ugly – beautiful
— Is Mary ugly?

g) slow – fast
— Are Japanese trains slow?

h) dirty – clean
— Are your hands dirty?

b) elderly – young
— Are they elderly?

i) square – round
— Is the Earth square?

c) sweet – sour
— Is lemon sweet?

j) short – long
— Is the sucuri snake short?

d) new – old
— Is Rome a new city?

k) light – heavy
   – Are elephants light?

l) cheap – expensive
   – Are these cars cheap?

ANOTAÇÕES

4. Dê respostas curtas na forma afirmativa ou negativa.

a) Are airplane slow? (no)

b) Is her house new? (yes)

c) Is this table clean? (yes)

d) Are these books expensive? (no)

e) Is Magali old? (no)

f) Is Marcel young? (no)

Lesson 3 – Definite article "the" – Indefinite article "a", "an"

The boy    The boys    The girl    The girls

USA-SE O ARTIGO DEFINIDO **THE**:

1) diante de substantivos com caráter específico, definido, exemplo:
   The ball in the box is mine.
   The cow in the barn is black.
2) diante de títulos, ex.:
   The president is absent.
3) diante de nomes de acidentes geográficos (montanhas, rios, mares etc.), ex.:
   The Andes, **The** Amazon, **The** Atlantic
4) diante de sobrenome de família, ex.:
   The Taylors are very gentle.
5) diante de nomes compostos de países, ex.:
   The United States
   The United Kingdom
   The Dominican Republic
6) diante de nomes de instrumentos musicais e danças, ex.:
   Mary plays **the** piano well.
   She dances **the** samba well.

1. De acordo com os exemplos acima, o artigo definido **the**:

   ( ) é invariável.
   ( ) varia do singular para o plural.
   ( ) varia do masculino para o feminino

2. Qual é o significado do artigo **the**?

NÃO SE USA O ARTIGO DEFINIDO THE

1) diante de substantivos usados em sentido geral, ex.:
   Children like ice cream.
   Cows are useful animals.

2) com nomes próprios, ex.:
   Jane is my friend.

3) com títulos acompanhados de nomes próprios, ex.:
   President Dilma is in Brasilia.

4) com nomes de esportes, disciplinas, continentes, países, estados, cidades, ex.:
   Football is my favorite sport.
   Geography is a science.
   Asia is a big continent.
   Brazil is a beautiful country.
   Bahia has beautiful beaches.

5) com as palavras **home** e **school**, ex.:
   She is at home.
   They are at school.
   I go to school.
   I come from home.

3. Complete as frases com o artigo **the** quando necessário.

a) _____ Brazilians like carnival.

b) _____ Water is a precious liquid.

c) _____ Alps are in Europe.

d) _____ Emily is a pretty girl.

e) _____ queen of England lives in London.

f) I like to play _____ piano.

g) Tourists like _____ Brazil.

h) _____ Canada is a rich country.

i) Trinidad and Tobago and _____ Dominican Republic are countries.

j) She lives in _____ United States.

k) _____ Rio is a marvelous city.

l) _____ Cavalcanti are a traditional family in Brazil.

m) _____ Dogs are domestic animals.

ARTIGO INDEFINIDO A (AN)

O artigo indefinido, em inglês, não tem plural e não varia do masculino para o feminino:

a boy (um menino)
 boys (meninos)
a girl (uma menina)
 girls (meninas)

Usa-se **an** diante de vogal e **h** mudo:

an animal • **an** apple • **an** elephant
an hour

4. Complete com **a** ou **an**.

a) This is ____ orange.

b) That is ____ big house.

c) That is ____ airplane.

d) He is ____ good friend.

e) This is ____ interesting book.

f) She is ____ old teacher.

g) He is ____ good doctor.

5. Escreva abaixo as frases anteriores no plural.

a)

b)

c)

d)

e)

f)

FUN TIME

1. Here's a challenge for you! What has a big head but doesn't think?

2. Read, think and discuss with your classmates:
What's the meaning of...

A long walk begins with an initial step.

WORD BANK
head: cabeça
cabbage: repolho
doesn't think: não pensa
walk: caminhada
begins: começa
step: passo

3. Complete com os artigos definidos e depois pinte a figura.

LITTLE PLUMBERS

NUMBER THE PICTURES THIS WAY
- Number 1 for   the   cat
- Number 2 for _____ broom
- Number 3 for _____ book
- Number 4 for _____ wrench
- Number 5 for _____ box of tools

COLOR THE PICTURE
Color   the   broom yellow
Color _____ cat brown
Color _____ wrench red
Color _____ rest as you like

WORD BANK
plumber: encanador
this way: deste modo
for: para
broom: vassoura

box: caixa
tools: ferramentas
wrench: chave de grifo, chave inglesa
as you like: como você quiser

Review – lessons 1, 2 and 3

1. Responda.

   a) What's your name?
      My name is

   b) What's your mother's name?
      My mother's name is

   c) What's your teacher's name?
      My teacher's name is

   d) What's your address?
      My address is

2. Veja a figura e responda.

   a) Are Jeff and Bob at school?

   b) Are they in a football field?

3. Responda em inglês.

   a) Are Brazilian beaches beautiful?

   b) Is sugar sour or sweet?

   c) Is honey sweet?

   d) Is lemon sweet or sour?

   e) Are Brazilian football players famous?

   f) Is the Amazon river short?

   g) Is your grandmother young?

4. Complete com o artigo **the** quando necessário. Observe o exemplo.

   The Amazon river is long.

a) _____ Atlantic ocean is very wide.

b) He plays _____ guitar very well.

c) She dances _____ reggae very well.

d) _____ president of Brazil is on vacation.

e) Are _____ United States a rich country?

5. Complete com **a** ou **an**.

a) I have _____ new bike.

b) This is _____ apple.

c) That is _____ red apple.

d) He is _____ old fisherman.

e) She is _____ good nurse.

6. Escreva no plural.

a) She is a good teacher.

b) He is my friend.

c) You are a famous singer.

d) I am an artist.

7. Observe as figuras e responda.

Is this an orange?

Is it a bird?

Are they musicians?

17

Lesson 4 – Ordinal numbers

ORDINAL NUMBERS

1st–first
2nd–second
3rd–third
4th–fourth
5th–fifth
6th–sixth
7th–seventh
8th–eighth
9th–ninth
10th–tenth
11th–eleventh
12th–twelfth
13th–thirteenth
14th–fourteenth
15th–fifteenth
16th–sixteenth
17th–seventeenth
18th–eighteenth
19th–nineteenth
20th–twentieth
21st–twenty-first
22nd–twenty-second
23rd–twenty-third
30th–thirtieth
40th–fortieth
50th–fiftieth

DAYS OF THE WEEK

Os dias da semana, em inglês, são escritos com letras iniciais maiúsculas.

Observe: Monday
Tuesday
Wednesday
Thursday
Friday
Saturday
Sunday

MONTHS

Também se escrevem com a letra inicial maiúscula.

January
February
March
April
May
June
July
August
September
October
November
December

1. Responda usando os numerais ordinais. Observe o exemplo.

What's the first month of the year?
The first month of the year is January.

a) What's the third month of the year?

b) What's the twelfth month of the year?

d) (fifth/May)

e) (sixth/June)

f) (seventh/July)

g) (eighth/August)

h) (ninth/September)

2. Observe o exemplo e continue.

(first/January)
January is the first month of the year.

a) (second/February)

b) (third/March)

c) (fourth/April)

i) (tenth/October)

j) (eleventh/November)

k) (twelfth/December)

3. Responda à pergunta.

What are the days of the week?

The days

4. Observe o exemplo e escreva os dias da semana pela ordem.

Monday is the first day of the week.

a) Tuesday

b)

c)

d)

e)

f)

5. Responda às perguntas. Observe o exemplo.

What is the first day of the week?
It's Monday.

a) What is the fourth day of the week?

b) What is the last day of the week?

c) For you, what is the best day of the week?

6. Observe o exemplo e escreva os meses do ano pela ordem.

January is the first month of the year.

a) February

b) March

c) April

d) May

e) June

f July

g) August

h) September

i) October

j) November

k) December

7. Responda às perguntas.

a) How many days are there in a week?

b) How many months are there in a year?

c) How many days are there in a month?

8. Reescreva a frase, colocando o dia e o mês do seu aniversário. Observe o exemplo.

My birthday is on the **(twenty-first)** of **(May)**.

9. Observe os exemplos e coloque a data de aniversário de alguns amigos ou amigas.

Pedro's birthday is on the tenth of December.

Mary's birthday is on the fifteenth of July.

a)

b)

c)

d)

10. Descubra quem é Roy Rogers.

WHICH ONE IS ROY ROGERS?

WANTED!
$5,000 REWARD
ROY ROGERS
TALL, THIN, BIG DARK MOUSTACHE, GREEN YELLOW NECKLACE, BIG HAT, LONG BOOTS, RED BELT.

Roy Rogers is:

( ) the first ( ) the third

( ) the second ( ) the fourth

11. Consulte o vocabulário no final do caderno e descubra qual destas palavras é o antônimo de **first**.

( ) next ( ) near
( ) last ( ) before

12. Traduza o texto do exercício 12 utilizando o vocabulário no final do caderno.

13. Observe a figura e responda.

a) Who's the first?

b) Who's the last?

c) Who's the third?

Dictation

14. Ouça com atenção o ditado que o professor vai apresentar e escreva.

FUN TIME

1. Look at the code and find out the secret message.

▽ = a   ⇨ = e   ❖ = k   ☐ = w

Tr▽v⇨l ▽nd ❖no☐ p⇨opl⇨,
n⇨☐ pl▽c⇨s, n⇨☐ lif⇨ styl⇨s
▽nd m▽❖e fri⇨nds.

The secret message is:

2. Complete the beginning or the ending of these words:

_____ ood   _____ ell
_____ eacher   studen _____
ho _____   clas _____
ca _____   _____ ad
_____ unday   yea _____

3. Complete a cruzada com os dias da semana, em inglês.

1. quinta-feira
2. domingo
3. quarta-feira
4. sexta-feira
5. terça-feira
6. sábado
7. segunda-feira

4. Show in the graph how much time you spend on homework and how much time you spend watching TV and then answer the questions below.

	H. Work	TV	H. Work	TV	H. Work	TV	H. Work	TV	H. Work	TV	H. Work	TV	H. Work	TV		H. Work	TV
180 min.																	
160 min.																	
140 min.																	
120 min.																	■
100 min.																	■
80 min.																	■
60 min.																■	■
40 min.																■	■
20 min.																■	■
	Monday		Tuesday		Wednesday		Thursday		Friday		Saturday		Sunday			Monday	

KEY: ■ minutes doing homework
     ■ minutes watching TV

↑ Example

a) How much time do you spend doing homework on Monday?
   I spend _____ minutes doing homework.

b) How much time do you spend watching TV on Monday?
   I spend _____ minutes doing homework.

c) How many minutes do you spend doing homework from Monday to Sunday?
   I spend _____ minutes.

d) How many minutes do you spend doing homework from Monday to Sunday?
   I spend _____ minutes.

e) On what day do you watch TV the most?
   On

f) On what day do you do the most homework?
   On

Lesson 5 – Verb to be – past tense (was/were)

– Hello!
– Hello! Karen, is your mother at home?
– No, she is not. She **was** here five minutes ago.

VERB TO BE – PAST TENSE

I was   (Eu era, estava ou fui, estive)
You were   (Você era, estava ou foi, esteve)
He was   (Ele era, estava ou foi, esteve)
She was   (Ela era, estava ou foi, esteve)
It was   (Ele, ela era, estava ou foi, esteve)
We were   (Nós éramos, estávamos ou fomos, estivemos)
You were   (Vocês eram, estavam ou foram, estiveram)
They were   (Eles, elas eram, estavam ou foram, estiveram)

1) As formas negativas do **past tense** de **to be** são:
   was not ou **wasn't** – **were not** ou **weren't**

2) Na forma interrogativa coloca-se o verbo antes do sujeito, exemplo:
   Was she in class?
   Were they your friends?

1. Complete com **was** ou **were**:

a) My sister _____ a good student.

b) John and his brother _____ farmers.

c) My parents _____ in the supermarket.

d) They _____ my friends.

e) She _____ at home and he _____ in the office.

f) We _____ hungry.

g) You _____ in the park last Sunday.

h) They _____ in my birthday party.

2. Observe o exemplo e escreva as frases:

(I – young / Now – old)
I was young. Now I am old.

a) (I – poor/ Now – rich)

b) (I – lazy / Now – hard-working)

c) (The room – clean / Now – dirty)

d) (The box – full / Now – empty)

e) (The teachers – strict / Now – kind)

f) (You – right / Now – wrong)

g) (We – thin / Now – fat)

3. Complete com o verbo **to be** no **simple past** e depois traduza.

Fred _____ unemployed last year but today he is very happy because he works in a big factory.

4. Complete com **am**, **is**, **are**, **was** ou **were**.

a) I _____ sick yesterday, but today I'm very well.

b) The teacher _____ late yesterday. The students _____ late too.

c) I _____ at home last night. My parents _____ too.

d) Today, you _____ busy. Yesterday you _____ too.

e) Jack _____ a student last year, but now he _____ a teacher.

f) The window _____ open now. Last night it _____ open too.

5. Escreva no **past tense**, em inglês.

a) Ela era muito feliz.

b) Eles estavam na festa.

c) Vocês foram bons estudantes.

d) Nós fomos amigos.

e) Você estava atrasado.

6. Passe para a forma negativa. Observe o exemplo.

She was my girlfriend.
She wasn't my girlfriend.

a) They were good friends.

b) Our parents were rich.

c) James was the president.

d) Mary was here last week.

e) They were in this city last year.

7. Who was...(Quem foi...)

William Shakespeare, English writer

Albert Einstein, German scientist

– Who was William Shakespeare?
– William Shakespeare was a famous English writer.

Ayrton Senna, Brazilian Formula 1 racer

Leonardo da Vinci, Italian painter

Machado de Assis, Brazilian writer

Pedro Álvares Cabral, Portuguese discoverer

8. Observe o exemplo e responda às perguntas.

Was Mary with you? (James)
No, she was not.
She was with James.

a) Were Jim and Lucy at the movies? (at a birthday party)

b) Were your parents at home? (at the shopping center.)

c) Was your mother sick? (well)

d) Were they rich? (poor)

9. Faça as perguntas para as respostas. Observe o exemplo.

Where were you?
I was at home.

b) _____
She was at school.

c) _____
They were well.

d) _____
My friends were with me.

10. Assinale a resposta certa.

a) Where were you yesterday?
( ) I was well.
( ) I was at the beach.
( ) I was alone.

b) How was she?
( ) She was not here.
( ) She was with you.
( ) She wasn't well.

11. Escreva no tempo passado.

a) They are at home.

b) The beach isn't clean.

c) It is a nice day.

d) They are good teachers.

e) I am well.

f) George isn't alone.

g) This restaurant is good.

h) The students are tired.

12. Complete as frases com **was** ou **were** e as expressões adverbais de tempo entre parênteses.

a) (yesterday)
What day is today?
What day _____

b) (last week)
She is here now, but _____ she _____ in Rio.

c) (two days ago)
_____ they _____ in Paris, but now they are in Brasília.

d) (two days ago)
Is it raining in Curitiba now?
No, but _____

e) (in 1997)
When _____ you born?

I _____ born in 1997.

13. Fill in the blanks with **was** or **were**.

Albert Einstein

Albert Einstein _____ born in 1879 in Germany. He _____ a son of Jervish family.
He _____ not a good student. His parents _____ worried about him. They thought that he _____ slow (stupid: not good at understanding things).
Albert Einstein is famous because he developed the theory of relativity. He _____ one of the most important scientists of the twentieth century.

Lesson 6 – There is... – there was...

Mother: Bill, there is a pudding in the refrigerator. Bring it to me.
Son: Oh, mother, **there was** a pudding...
Mother: There was?...
Son: Yes, **there was**...
Mother: ?...

THERE TO BE – PRESENT TENSE

Singular:
   There is a boy in the class. (Há um menino na classe.)

Plural:
   There are seven boys in the class. (Há sete alunos na sala.)

THERE TO BE – PAST TENSE

O verbo haver, no passado, possui duas formas:
   a) **There was**, usada no singular:
      There was a boy in the class. (Havia um menino na classe.)
   b) **There were**, usada no plural:
      There were boys in the class. (Havia meninos na classe.)

1. Complete o diálogo com o verbo **to be** no tempo passado. Use as formas **was** ou **were**.

– Where _____ you last week?
– I _____ in Rio.
– _____ you at the beach?
– Yes, I _____ .
– What beach?
– Copacabana beach.
– _____ the Copacabana beach clean?
– Yes, it _____ very clean.
– What is the name of the hotel you _____ in?
– I _____ at Copacabana Palace.
– _____ there many tourists?
– Yes, there _____ many tourists from many parts of the world.

2. Traduza o diálogo que você completou no exercício anterior.

3. Compare a figura da direita com a da esquerda e forme frases de acordo com o exemplo. Empregue **there was** ou **there were** – **there are** ou **there is**.

There were six birds on the tree.   Now there are only three.

4. Complete com **there was** ou **there were**.

a) _____ a garden in front of the house.

b) _____ strict teachers in my school.

c) _____ beautiful girls in the party.

d) _____ a good reason to go home.

5. Escreva no **past tense**. Observe o exemplo.

How many people are there in this room?
How many people were there in this room?

How many boys and girls are there in the party?

6. Escreva em inglês.

a) Quantas pessoas havia na sala?

b) Quantas crianças havia no parque?

c) Quantas mulheres havia naquela sala?

7. Observe o exemplo e escreva as frases.

(10 oranges / in the box / 6)
There were ten oranges in the box, but now there are only six.

a) (50 dollars / in the wallet / 5)

b) (15 birds / on the tree / 2)

c) He was an old farmer.

d) She was a beautiful girl.

8. Escreva no **past tense**.

a) I am a teacher.

b) We are teachers.

c) I am poor, but happy.

9. Preencha a cruzadinha com os ordinais.

10. Preencha a cruzadinha com os números correspondetes em inglês.

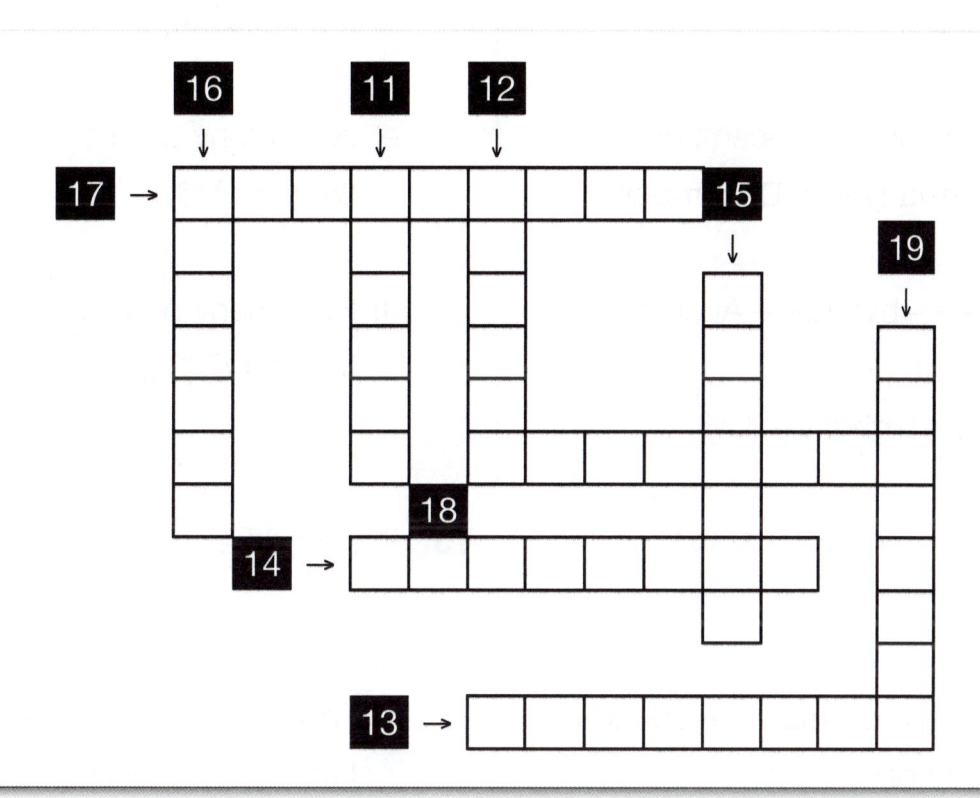

11. Complete os dias da semana na ordem.

September - 2012	Sunday						
							1
	2	3	4	5	6	7	8
	9	10	11	12	13	14	15
	16	17	18	19	20	21	22
	23	24	25	26	27	28	29
	30						

12. Complete os meses do ano na tabela abaixo.

February	August
April	October
June	December

13. Observe o exemplo e escreva em inglês.

My – birthday – December
My birthday is in December.

a) Your – birthday – August

b) His – birthday – July

c) Her – birthday – March

14. Observe o exemplo e responda às questões.

How many boys are there in your classroom? (15)
There are fifteen boys in my classroom.

a) How many girls are there in your classroom? (14)

b) How many bedrooms are there in your house? (3)

c) How many states are there in Brazil? (26)

d) How many apples were there on the table? (4)

e) How many babies were there in the park? (6)

f) How many people were there in the party? (30)

15. Responda às questões.

a) How old are you?
I'm _____ years old.
I am _____ years old.

b) How many brothers and sisters do you have?
I have _____ brothers and sisters.

c) And you, how many friends do you have?
I have _____ friends.

16. Complete.

Ten plus ten is
Forty divided by eight is
Sixty-six minus twenty is

Ten times two is

17. Complete com **was** ou **were**.

a) It _____ very cold yesterday morning.
b) She _____ my first friend at school.
c) We _____ at the beach last month.
d) Where _____ you last night?
e) I _____ at George's house.

18. Complete com o verbo **to be** no tempo passado, na forma afirmativa ou negativa.

a) They _____ at home last night. (negative)
b) The school _____ near my house. (affirmative)
c) She _____ well. (negative)
d) The boys _____ playing football. (affirmative)
e) Some girls _____ present at school. (negative)

19. Mude para o tempo passado.

a) She is my teacher.

b) The nurses are in the hospital.

c) It is a wonderful night.

d) We are at home.

Dictation

20. Ouça com atenção o ditado que o professor vai apresentar e escreva.

Lesson 7 – Prepositions – I

my book Buscar   Início Perfil Mensagens

Fred

Hi, John!
What about going to the Teens Sport Club tomorrow?
Let's take part in the football competition.
I like football very much. It's my favorite sport.
After the game we can eat a sandwich in the snack bar. OK?

Bye
Fred

John

Hi, Fred!
That's a good idea! I like football, too.
The competition in the club is great!
I don't want to miss that!
Wait for me tomorrow in front of the club.
Don't forget your shorts and football boots!
See you tomorrow.
John.

Do you like sports? Come to our competition in the club.

Competition timetable
October and November

M = in the morning   A = in the afternoon
From 9 to 12 a.m.   From 3 to 6 p.m.

On **Monday**	On **Wednesday**	On **Friday**	On **Saturday**
Football M	Swinning M	Handball M A	Football M
Volleyball A	Basketball M	Roller skating	Table tennis A
Cycling A	Running A	Bowling A	Athletics M A

38

1. Traduza um dos e-mails.

2. Veja o **Timetable** anterior e crie novos jogos e horários para o campeonato do Teens Sport Club, nos dias que estavam sem jogos.

Competition timetable
_____ and _____

M = in the morning A = in the afternoon
From ____ to ____ a.m.   From ____ to ____ p.m.

Monday	Tuesday	Wednesday	Thursday	Friday	Saturday
Football M	_____	Swinning M	_____	Handball M A	Football M
Volleyball A	_____	Basketball M	_____	Roller skating	Table tennis A
Cycling A	_____	Running A	_____	Bowling A	Athletics M A
On	On	On	On	On	On

March comes **before** April.
April comes **after** March.

PREPOSITIONS

Before (antes):
Saturday comes **before** Sunday.
(Sábado vem antes de domingo.)
After (depois):
Sunday comes **after** Saturday.
(Domingo vem depois de sábado.)
On, **at**:
Observe o emprego de **on** com dias da semana e **at** com as horas:
On Saturday **at** six o'clock.
No sábado, às seis horas.
In (em, dentro de):
The water is **in** a glass.

On (sobre, em cima de):
The book is **on** the table.
Under (sob, embaixo de):
The cat is **under** the chair.
Of (de):
A book **of** English.
A cup **of** tea.

Expressões:
On the right: à direita
On the left: à esquerda
At home: em casa
At school: na escola

1. Before/after

Responda às perguntas.
Observe o exemplo.

What day of the week comes before Sunday?
It's Saturday.

a) What day of the week comes after Monday?

b) What day of the week comes before Friday?

c) What day of the week comes after Tuesday?

2. Responda as perguntas.
Observe o exemplo.

Is February after or before January? (after)
February is after January.

a) Is June after or before July? (before)

b) Is October before or after September? (after)

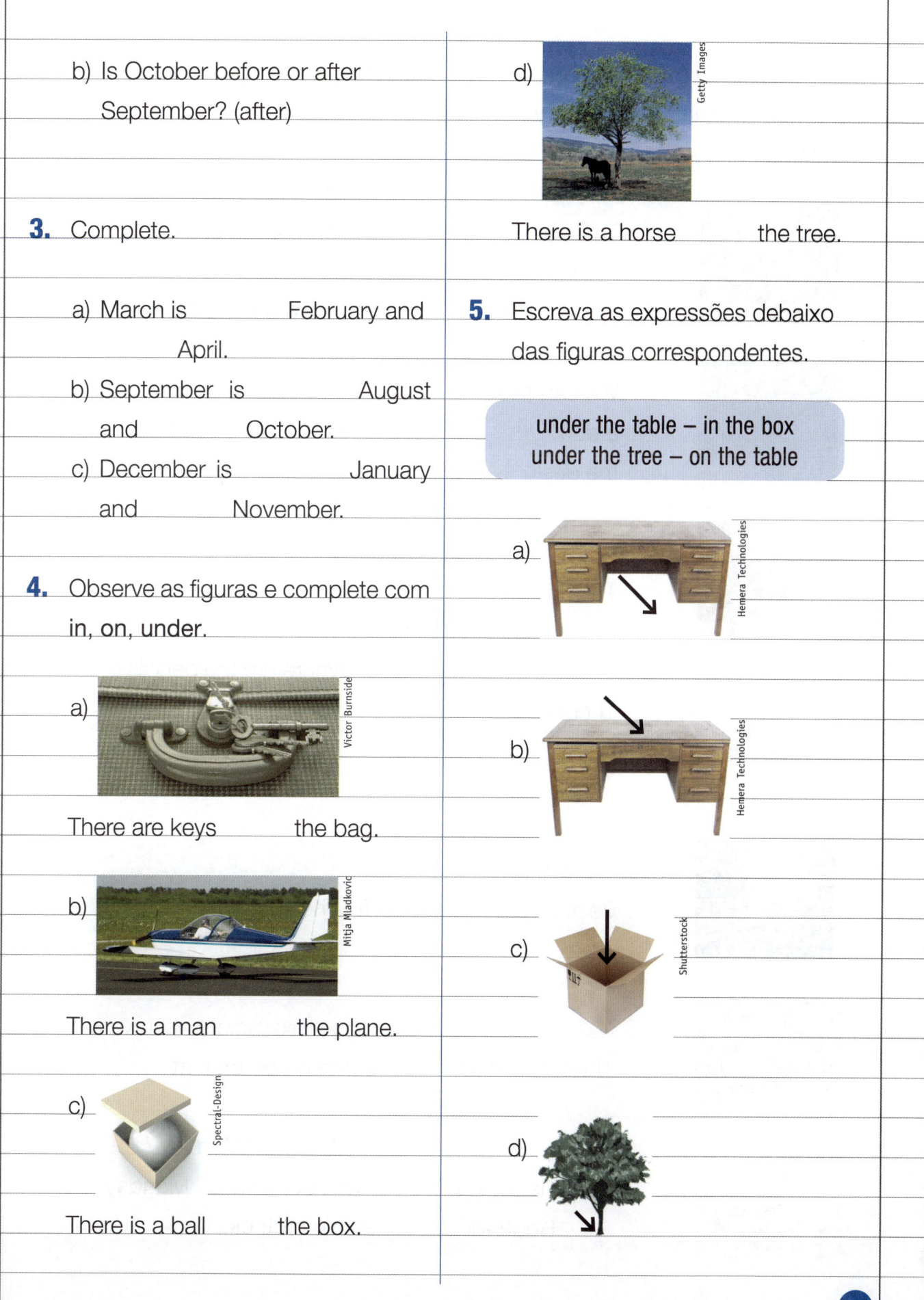

3. Complete.

a) March is _____ February and _____ April.
b) September is _____ August and _____ October.
c) December is _____ January and _____ November.

4. Observe as figuras e complete com **in, on, under**.

a) There are keys _____ the bag.

b) There is a man _____ the plane.

c) There is a ball _____ the box.

d) There is a horse _____ the tree.

5. Escreva as expressões debaixo das figuras correspondentes.

under the table – in the box
under the tree – on the table

a)

b)

c)

d)

6. Complete as frases com **in, on, under, with** e ligue-as às figuras correspondentes:

There are roses ____ the vase.

We can see a dog ____ the desk.

There is a vase ____ the table.

There is a purse ____ the desk.

We can see pencils ____ a box.

There is a map ____ the wall.

Paula is sitting ____ Roberto.

7. Observe as figuras ao lado e responda.

Where is the vase?
It is on the table.

a) Where are the flowers?

b) Where is the dog?

c) Where is the purse?

d) Where are the pencils?

e) Is Paula sitting with Roberto?

f) Where is the map?

8. Siga o exemplo e observe o emprego de **on** e **at**:

I / at home / Monday / 5
I was at home on Monday at five o'clock.

a) He / at home / Tuesday / 6

b) She / at the party / Wednesday / 7

c) I / at the movies / Friday / 9

9. Escreva **true** (verdadeiro) ou **false** (falso).

(   ) January comes before February.
(   ) April comes after May.
(   ) Saturday comes before Sunday.

10. Complete com **after** ou **before**.

The policeman is running _____ the thief.

11. Verificar a figura para poder responder.

Is there a cat **under** the table?
No, there is not.
The cat is on the table.

a) Is there a girl **on** the chair?

b) Is there a man **in** the car?

Lesson 8 – Prepositions – II

Fred is a cowboy from Texas.

He works in a big farm for a rich farmer.

He works for many hours every day.

Now, he is between two cows.

PREPOSITIONS

From (de)
  From indica origem, procedência, começo:
  a) I come **from** France.
  b) This cheese is **from** Minas.

To (para)
  To indica destino, fim de uma ação:
  a) I go **to** Rio.
  b) Give the book **to** him.
  c) I work **from** one **to** seven o'clock.

For (para, por)
  For indica posse eventual, duração de tempo:
  a) Here is a present **for** you.
  b) She was here **for** many weeks.

Between (entre dois seres ou dois grupos de seres)
  I am **between** Mary and John.

Among (entre, no meio de muitos)
  I am **among** friends.

With (com)
  a) I go **with** you.
  b) Come **with** me.

Without (sem)
  Don't go out **without** money.

Up (para cima) **Down:** (para baixo)

This singer is **between** a lot of fans.

1. Complete as frases com as preposições from, to, for, between, among, with, without.

a) Where are you coming _____ ?
b) I'm coming _____ Rio.
c) He comes _____ Rio _____ São Paulo.

d) God be _____ you.

e) I was at home _____ my mother.

f) The teacher treats all the students equally _____ distinction.

g) That politician likes to be _____ many people.

h) It's about 400 (four hundred) kilometers _____ São Paulo _____ Rio.

i) This present is _____ you.

j) I was there _____ a long time.

k) I go to your party _____ my family.

l) Can I go _____ you?

2. Complete as frases com as preposições adequadas, de acordo com a foto abaixo. Use **in, on, under, at, with, for, between, among**.

Meg's birthday

Meg's birthday was _____ Saturday _____ seven o'clock. _____ the room there were many things and people.
We can see _____ the picture Meg _____ a present.
We can see a boy _____ two friends. There is a cake _____ the table.

3. Complete o diálogo a seguir com as preposições do quadro abaixo.

> between – to – in – with
> of – on – at

– Good morning!
– Good morning!
– Please, come _____ !
– Thank you.
(Mary enters the house _____ her children Rony and Flavia.)
– Let's go _____ the living room. Please sit down _____ this sofa and make yourself _____ home.
– Thank you.
Mary is _____ her children Rony and Flavia. Rony is _____ the right _____ his mother and Flavia is _____ the left.

4. Complete as frases e a cruzadinha e descubra a palavra escondida (hidden word).

a) em, dentro de
   (The boy is _____ the car.)

b) entre (dois)
   (I'm _____ Mary and John.)

c) de (origem)
   (He is _____ Rio.)

d) com
   (I live _____ my parents.)

HIDDEN WORD ↓

a) _____ W _____
b) _____ _____ _____ _____ _____ _____
c) _____ _____ H _____
d) _____ _____ U _____

What's the hidden word?
It's _____ .

Lesson 9 – Verb can (verbo poder)

CAN

Can não recebe **s** na 3ª pessoa do singular, exemplo:

He **can** (Ele pode).

Can não tem infinitivo, portanto não se pode dizer **to can**.

Can significa poder ou saber fazer alguma coisa.

I **can** lift the bag.
(Eu posso levantar a mala.)
Can you drive?
(Você sabe dirigir?)

A forma negativa é **can't** ou **cannot**.

> Can you help me?
> Sure, we can!

1. Observe o vocabulário no final do caderno e relacione adequadamente os verbos aos substantivos.

a) love   finger
b) lick   heart
c) think   nose
d) point   head
e) smell   tongue
f) speak   legs
g) touch   mouth
h) walk   ears
i) see   eyes
j) hear   hands

2. Baseado no exercício acima, forme frases de acordo com o exemplo.

I can love with my heart.

a) I can lick

b)

c)

d)

e)

f)

g)

h)

i)

3. Baseado nos exercícios anteriores, complete as frases com substantivos.

a) You can see with your
b) She can touch with her
c) Bob can speak with his   .
d) I can walk with my   .
e) She can love with her
f) You can smell with your
g) We can see with our
h) I can love with my

4. Complete as frases com verbos.

a) You can   with your legs.
b) I can   with my tongue.
c) We can   with our eyes.
d) We can   with our ears.

5. Responda às perguntas. Observe o exemplo.

What can you do with your legs?
I can walk. I can run.
I can dance...

a) What can you do with your eyes?

b) What can you do with your hands?

c) What can you do with your nose?

d) What can we do with our legs?

e) What can you do with your head?

f) What can she do with her heart?

6. Responda **Yes or no**. Observe os exemplos.

Can you ride a horse? (y)
Yes, I can.

Can you drive a bus? (n)
No, I can't.

48

a) Can you drive a car? (y)

b) Can you row a boat? (n)

c) Can you fly an airplane? (n)

d) Can you ride a bicycle? (y)

e) Can you speak Japanese? (n)

f) Can they help you? (n)

g) Can Mary drive a bus? (n)

h) Can John speak Italian? (y)

i) Can John and Rose speak Japanese? (n)

7. We can make many things from the wood of the trees.
Observe o exemplo e coloque os objetos no plural.

chair

We can make chairs.

a) door

b) a pencil

c) a fence

d) a table

e) a boat

f) a ruler

WORD BANK
can: podemos **many:** muitas
from: de (origem) **of:** de
(to) make: fazer **things:** coisas
wood: madeira **tree:** árvore

Review – lessons 7, 8 and 9

1. Veja as figuras e faça frases em inglês usando **in**, **on**, **under**. Observe o exemplo.

car – tree

The car is under the tree.

book – table

a)

cat – bed

b)

2. Passe para o inglês.

a) Estive no Pará por duas semanas.

b) Eu sou de Manaus e você é do Rio.

c) Este queijo é de Minas?

d) Havia laranjas na cesta.

e) Os professores estão entre os estudantes.

f) Eu estava entre Mary e John.

3. Preencha com **after** ou **before**.

a) Monday comes _____ Sunday.

b) Saturday comes _____ Sunday.

c) January comes _____ February.

d) March comes _____ February.

4. Observe o exemplo e continue.

My class / 8 / Monday

My class begins at 8 o'clock on Monday.

a) Your class / 9 / Monday

50

b) My work / 7 / Tuesday

c) This TV program / 10 / Saturday

5. Escreva as frases embaixo das figuras correspondentes.

a) John can't swim.
b) I can swim.
c) Bob can't walk now.
d) The baby can walk now.

6. Passe para a forma negativa. Observe o exemplo.

She can walk.
She can't walk.

a) I can see.

b) I can read.

c) The old man can run.

7. Complete as frases com a preposição correta.

a) I came _____ Rio. (from/in)

b) They are _____ friends. (in/among)

c) You are _____ Mexico. (to/from/in)

d) We go _____ you. (with/ from)

e) You are _____ Paul and Peter. (among/between)

f) This present is _____ you. (with/for/among)

51

g) They are _____ Recife. (with/from)

h) He plans to stay in Paris _____ a month. (to/in/for)

i) She was in Rio _____ many weeks. (in/for)

j) I was born _____ Monday, _____ the morning, _____ August, 1997. (in/for/on/from)

8. Escreva em inglês.

a) Estive em Salvador por uma semana.

b) Havia um tomate na geladeira.

c) Os tomates estão entre as batatas.

9. Follow the patterns and write the sentences.

a) Picture
   What can you see in the picture?

b) Photograph

c) Room

d) What can you see in the picture? (four boys)
   I can see four boys.

e) What can you see in the picture? (a boy)

f) What can you see in the picture? (three birds)

10. Responda às perguntas.

a) Were your parents at home yesterday night? (at the movies)

b) Was Grace at home this morning? (at the supermarket)

FUN TIME

Curiosities

Birthday Song and cards.

ABOUT BIRTHDAY SONGS

The *Happy Birthday* song is more than one hundred years old.

It was written in 1893 by two sisters, Patty and Mildred Hill, who were school teachers in Louisville, Kentucky.

Fonte: www.birthdaycelebrations.net/birthdaysong.htm.
Acessado em 16/01/2013

ABOUT BIRTHDAY CARDS

The tradition of sending birthday cards started in England about 100 years ago.

Fonte: www.birthdaycelebrations.net/birthdaycards.htm.
Acessado em 16/01/2013

WORD BANK
was written: foi escrito
were: eram
Kentucky: Um estado dos Estados Unidos.
started: começou

1. Escreva números de 1 a 9, sem repetir, de modo a obter os totais. A challenge for you! Find out the numbers.

Write the numbers from 1 to 9 in each empty box.

			14
			14
			17
16	14	15	16

ANOTAÇÕES

c) Were you at the birthday party? (at the football game)

d) Was Carol your first girlfriend? (Monica)

11. Complete as frases, com as preposições in, on ou at.

1. I go to school ____ the morning.
2. Do you live ____ Brazil?
3. She was born ____ Paris.
4. My birthday is ____ May.
5. I get up ____ 7 o'clock.
6. I always wash my car ____ Mondays.
7. The restaurant is ____ the right side of the road.
8. My classroom is ____ the second floor.
9. Every time i get ____ the bus, it is full of people.
10. She is ____ home now.
11. Where's Mary? She is ____ school.
12. Pay attention ____ the crossroads!
13. It is cold ____ winter.
14. Put the pencils ____ the box, please.
15. Where's my wallet? It is ____ your pocket.
16. Where's my money? It is ____ your wallet.
17. How do you go to school? ____ foot or by bus?
18. She likes to watch soap operas ____ TV.
19. I live ____ the 7th floor, ____ 25 Britain Street ____ London.
20. ____ the entrance of the city, there is a sign: Drive slowly.

A game for you

Aluno, você e um colega podem se divertir e treinar um pouco mais o seu inglês. Se precisarem, usem o vocabulário do final do livro. Para jogar, usem um dado ou façam um de cartolina.

WORD BANK
Start: comece
go to: vá para
go back: volte
miss a turn: perde a vez
miss one throw: perde um lance
tortoise: tartaruga

- START HERE
- Dog house
- Go to the cat's basket.
- Miss a turn.
- Go to the Pet Shop.
- Cat's basket
- Go back to the house of the dog.
- PET SHOP
- You can go on two spaces.
- Go to the tortoise.
- Go to the rabbit.
- Tortoise
- Miss one throw.
- Go back to the mouse.
- Go back to the Pet Shop.
- FINISH!

Lesson 10 – Could, could not

- Please could you tell me where Alabama street is?
- Sure. Go straight ahead. Alabama street crosses this street at the traffic lights.
- Thank you.
- You're welcome.

Could significa podia ou poderia:

I **could** help you.

Could you tell me the time?

A forma negativa de **could** é **could not** ou **couldn't**.

Could é bastante usado para fazer pedidos:

Could I use your telephone?

1. Traduza o diálogo acima.

2. Mude para o tempo passado. Observe o exemplo.

She **can** help you.
She could help you.

a) **Can** you take my bag?

b) **Can** I use your telephone?

c) You **can** go to the party.

d) You **can** pay the bill.

e) They **can** speak English.

f) I **can** go by car.

g) They **can** hear you.

3. Escreva um diálogo sobre alguém que pede informação na rua. Veja no Word bank as palavras que você pode usar.

WORD BANK
Where can I buy...?: Onde eu posso comprar...?
Can you help me?: Você pode ajudar-me?
walk: caminhe
go: vá
straight: reto
straight ahead: reto em frente
turn right: vire à direita
turn left: vire à esquerda
two blocks: dois quarteirões
till: até
bus stop: parada de ônibus
book store: livraria
library: biblioteca
Bank of Brazil: Banco do Brasil
post office: correio
church of...: igreja de...
supermarket: supermercado
square: praça
bus station: estação de ônibus
airport: aeroporto
drugstore: farmácia

4. A forma verbal **could**, no tempo passado, é usada com frequência para expressar polidez e delicadeza quando solicitamos algo de alguém. Destaque do exercício anterior duas frases que denotam essa ideia.

5. Passe para a forma negativa abreviada. Observe o exemplo.

I **could** hear you.
I **couldn't** hear you.

a) She **could** speak English.

b) I **can** tell the secret.

c) Bob **could** lift that stone.

d) I **could** help you.

e) I **can** walk.

f) I **could** see the airplane.

g) She **can** play tennis with her friend.

h) She **could** dance with you.

6. Observe o exemplo e escreva na forma interrogativa. Acrescente a palavra **please** nas perguntas em que a pessoa pede um favor.

She can sing at the party.
Can she sing at the party?

a) You could help me.

b) You can speak English.

c) You could take my bags.

d) You could hear me for a moment.

e) They can read magazines.

7. What can you see in the picture?

1. I can see the   .
2. I can see a girl with a   .
3. I can see a boy with a   .
4. I can see a   .
5. I can see a   .
6. I can see a boy with a   .
7. I can see the blue   .

Observe o exemplo, faça a pergunta e responda.

What can you see in the picture?
(see number one)
I can see the sky.

a)
     (see number two)

b)
     (see number three)

c)
     (see number four)

d)
     (see number five)

e)
     (see number six)

f)
     (see number seven)

8. Name the **things** and the **people** that appear in the picture.

Things	People

59

Lesson 11 – Simple present

MY EVERYDAY ROUTINE

I am in the seventh grade.

I get up at six every day, take a shower, get dressed, have breakfast and brush my teeth.

I leave home at seven, take a bus and go to school.

My classes start at eight o'clock.

SIMPLE PRESENT TENSE (PRESENTE SIMPLES)

Os verbos do texto acima estão no presente simples ou presente do indicativo. Estes verbos indicam ações que se fazem costumeiramente, que se repetem.

1) Observe a conjugação do verbo **to take** (tomar) no **simple present tense**:

I take	(Eu tomo)	We take	(Nós tomamos)
You take	(Você toma)	You take	(Vocês tomam)
He take**s**	(Ele toma)	They take	(Eles/Elas tomam)
She take**s**	(Ela toma)		

2) Observe a conjugação do verbo **to brush** (escovar) no **simple present tense**:

I brush	(Eu escovo)	We brush	(Nós escovamos)
You brush	(Você escova)	You brush	(Vocês escovam)
He brush**es**	(Ele escova)	They brush	(Eles/Elas escovam)
She brush**es**	(Ela escova)		

3) Observe que, assim como **to brush** (escovar), os verbos terminados em **s**, **sh**, **ch**, **o**, **x** são conjugados acrescentando-se **es** na 3ª pessoa do singular. Exemplo: to pa**s**s (passar), to wa**sh** (lavar), to tea**ch** (ensinar), to g**o** (ir), to fix etc. (passes, washes, teaches, goes, fixes).

4) Observe:
   a) Nos verbos terminados em **y** precedido de **vogal**, acrescenta-se **s** na 3ª pessoa do singular, exemplo: I say / He say**s** (Eu digo / Ele diz).
   b) Nos verbos terminados em **y** precedido de **consoante**, muda-se o **y** por **ies** na 3ª pessoa do singular, exemplo: I try / She tr**ies** (Eu tento / Ela tenta).

1. Traduza o texto "My everyday routine".

2. Coloque as ações do texto na ordem cronológica.

I take a shower.
I have breakfast.
I get up at six o'clock.

3. Escreva o exercício 2 na 3ª pessoa do singular do presente do indicativo. Use os pronomes **he** ou **she**.

He takes a shower.
She has breakfast.

4. Que outras terminações verbais recebem **es** na 3ª pessoa do singular do presente do indicativo?

Pesquise exemplos.

5. Como fica a 3ª pessoa do singular do presente do indicativo dos verbos terminados em y precedido de vogal?

Pesquise exemplos.

6. E os verbos terminados em y precedido de consoante?

Pesquise exemplos.

7. Observe a conjugação dos verbos **to take** (tomar, pegar) e **to brush** (escovar), e responda.

Em que pessoa verbal ocorre um acréscimo com relação às outras pessoas verbais?

Qual foi o acréscimo?

8. Escreva os verbos na 3ª pessoa do singular do presente do indicativo: Use os pronomes **he**, **she** ou **it**.

I sing. (Eu canto.) **She sings**. (Ela canta.)

a) I play. (Eu brinco, eu jogo.)

b) They speak. (Eles falam.)

c) They fly. (Eles voam.)

d) I fish. (Eu pesco.)

9. Conjugue os verbos **to reach** (alcançar) e **to go** (ir) no **simple present tense**.

I reach   I go

10. Conjugue o verbo **to play** (jogar) no **simple present tense**.

11. Conjugue o verbo **to study** (estudar) no **simple present tense**.

12. Passe as frases para a 3ª pessoa do singular.

They go to the school in the morning. (He)
He goes to the school in the morning.

a) I study English every day. (She)

b) I get up at seven o'clock. (He)

c) I brush my teeth after the meals. (She)

d) The trains reach the station at night.

e) You go to school in the morning. (He)

f) They take the bus at seven o'clock. (He)

g) They play football on Sundays. (He)

> **Observação:**
>
> O verbo **to have** (ter) forma a 3ª pessoa do singular do presente do indicativo de forma irregular:
> I have (Eu tenho)
> You have (Você tem)
> He **has** (Ele tem)
> She **has** (Ela tem)
> We have (Nós temos)
> You have (Vocês têm)
> They have (Eles/Elas têm)

13. Preencha as lacunas com **have** ou **has**.

a) I _____ breakfast at 8 o'clock.

b) She _____ many friends.

c) We _____ four meals a day.

d) Mary _____ two brothers.

e) They _____ some problems.

14. Resolva a cruzada usando verbos na 3ª pessoa do singular do presente do indicativo:

1) to study
2) to dance
3) to reach
4) to have
5) to play
6) to say
7) to rush
8) to cross
9) to sit
10) to take
11) to speak
12) to smile

Dictation

15. Ouça com atenção o ditado que o professor vai apresentar e escreva.

Lesson 12 – Present continuous tense

Suzy: Hello, Monica!
Monica: Hello, Suzy!
Suzy: Are your children at home?
Monica: No, they aren't.
Richard is going to your house.
George is playing football.
Lucy is running in the park.
Suzy: Ok, Monica. Thank you. Bye!

1. Traduza o diálogo.

PRESENT CONTINUOUS TENSE

George **is playing** football now.
(George está jogando futebol agora.)

O **present continuous** indica uma ação que está sendo realizada agora, que começou e continua se realizando ainda.
O **present continuous** é formado pelo verbo **to be** (estar), no presente, mais o gerúndio do verbo principal.

SIMPLE PRESENT TENSE

George **plays** football on Sundays.
(Jorge joga futebol aos domingos.)

O verbo acima indica o que George faz costumeiramente.
O **simple present tense** indica uma ação que se repete, que se faz costumeiramente.

GERUND

Forma-se o gerúndio, em inglês, acrescentando-se a terminação **ing** ao verbo:

play + ing = play**ing** (jogando);

eat + ing = eat**ing** (comendo).

Os verbos terminados em **e** perdem o **e**:
danc~~e~~ + ing = danc**ing** (dançando).

Alguns verbos dobram a consoante final:
run + ing = ru**nn**ing (correndo).

stop + ing = sto**pp**ing (parando).

begin + ing = begi**nn**ing (começando).

2. Escreva os verbos no gerúndio.
(**to go: going**)

a) to sleep:
b) to study:
c) to play:
d) to speak:
e) to dance:
f) to sing:
g) to work:
h) to run:
i) to take:

3. Conjugue o verbo **to work** (trabalhar) no **simple present tense**.

I
You
He/She/It
We
You
They

4. Conjugue o verbo **to work** (trabalhar) no **present continuous tense**.

I
You
He/She/It
We
You
They

5. Observe o exemplo e responda usando gerúndio.

What are you doing?
(to plant / a tree)
I am planting a tree.

a) What is she doing?
(to read / a book)

b) What are they doing?
(to play / football)

c) What are the girls doing?
(to sing)

d) What is the man doing?
(to drive / a car)

e) What are you doing?
(to study / Geography)

6. Observe o exemplo e escreva os diálogos.

Richard – go home
– **What is Richard doing?**
– **Richard is going home.**

a) George – play football

b) Lucy – run in the park

c) Mary – do her homework

7. Monte frases com as palavras fornecidas.

a) talking – is – dentist – to the – Kate

b) are – Mara – Betty – studying – and – Science

c) park – the boys – the girls – and in – running – the – are

d) writing – the teacher – is – on board – the

8. Separe as palavras e forme frases. Observe o exemplo.

Iamwritingastory.
I am writing a story.

a) Theyareplayingbasketball.

b) Thebabiesaresleeping.

c) Whatareyouwashing?

d) Thegirlsaresinginganddancing.

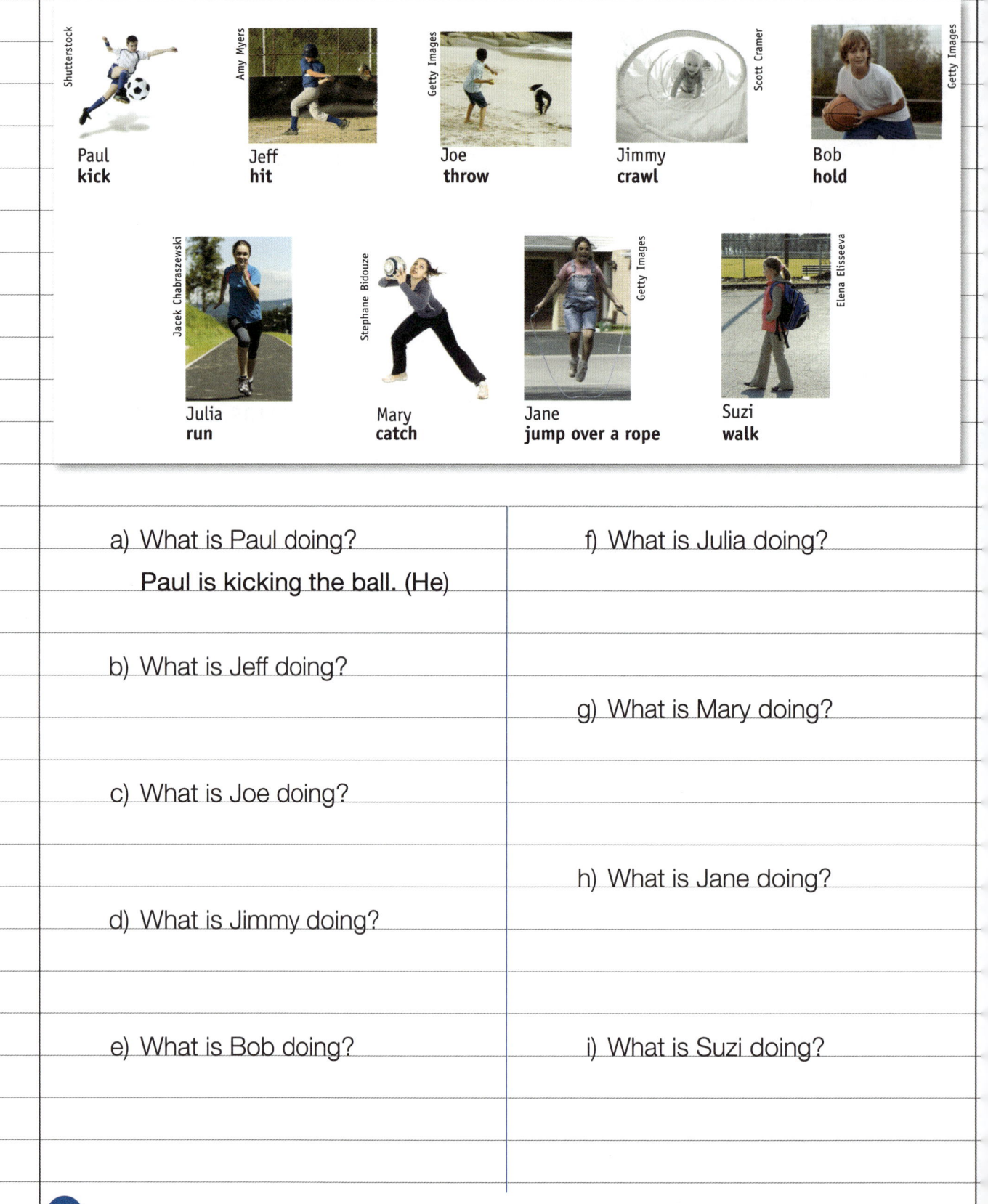

9. Observe os diversos tipos de ação nas figuras e responda às perguntas. Observe o exemplo.

Paul — **kick**
Jeff — **hit**
Joe — **throw**
Jimmy — **crawl**
Bob — **hold**

Julia — **run**
Mary — **catch**
Jane — **jump over a rope**
Suzi — **walk**

a) What is Paul doing?
  Paul is kicking the ball. (He)

b) What is Jeff doing?

c) What is Joe doing?

d) What is Jimmy doing?

e) What is Bob doing?

f) What is Julia doing?

g) What is Mary doing?

h) What is Jane doing?

i) What is Suzi doing?

10. Observe os diversos tipos de ação na figura e responda às perguntas. Observe o exemplo.

Janet	Jack	Louis	Monica
drop	**climb**	**fall**	**pull**

Joseph	Nick	Jim
hide	**push**	**put**

a) What is Janet doing?
   (to drop a book)
   Janet is dropping a book.
   ou (She is dropping a book).

b) What is Jack doing?
   (to climb a tree)

c) What is Louis doing?
   (to fall from the net)

d) What is Monica doing?
   (to pull the cart)

e) What is Joseph doing?
   (to hide behind a tree)

f) What is Albert doing?
   (to push Nick in a skate)

g) What is Jim doing?
   (to put down the bucket)

11. Observe o modelo e responda às peguntas.

What are you planting? (flowers)
I am planting flowers.

a) What are you drinking? (milk)

b) What are they studying? (History)

c) What are you washing? (my hands)

d) What are you brushing? (my teeth)

e) What is the teacher teaching? (English)

12. Observe o exemplo e faça a pergunta.

Who is dancing? (Mary)
Mary is dancing.

a)
    The boy is going to school. (the boy)

b)
    The teacher is running in the park. (the theacher)

c)
    My father is drinking coffee. (my father)

d)
    Jane is calling you. (Jane)

e)
    My friend is crossing the street. (my friend)

13. Passe para o plural. Observe o exemplo.

I am working.
We are working.

a) The boy is going to school.

b) The baby is sleeping.

c) She is painting.

d) You are playing tennis.

e) That beautiful woman is dancing.

f) He is singing.

h) You are studying.

g) I am walking to school.

14. Desenhe figuras de acordo com as frases.

These boys are playing football.

These girls are dancing.

15. Observe o exemplo e escreva os diálogos.

you wash the plates / glasses – Are you washing the plates? – No, I am washing the glasses. a) she – read – a magazine/newspaper	b) they – drink – water/orange juice c) they – play – tennis/football

16. Utilizando as palavras do quadro, monte substantivos compostos debaixo das respectivas figuras.

foot / motor / ball / flower / tooth / sun
cycle / ice / brush / police / man / cream

Dictation

17. Ouça com atenção o ditado que o professor vai apresentar e escreva.

ANOTAÇÕES

Review – lessons 13 and 14

1. Escreva as no passado. Observe o exemplo.

I **can** help you.
I **could help you.**

a) I **can** speak English.

b) She can write the letter.

c) Mr Porter can repair the watch.

d) You can read this book.

e) They can go with you.

f) He can get up early.

g) The acrobats can walk on the rope.

h) The dogs can jump over that box.

i) She can drive the car.

2. Complete as frases com as palavras abaixo.

> football player – singer
> driver – teacher

a) Bill sings very well.
   He is a _____.

b) Bob drives fast.
   He is a _____.

c) Alan plays football every day.
   He is a _____.

d) Alice teaches English.
   She is an English _____.

3. Ligue os verbos aos substantivos.

the cook • • teaches
the teacher • • plays
the student • • cooks
the player • • sings
the singer • • studies
the farmer • • works
the worker • • builds
the engineer • • plants

4. Assinale a alternativa correta.

a) Who paints houses?
( ) the cook
( ) the nurse
( ) the painter

b) Who lives on a farm?
( ) the singer
( ) the farmer
( ) the doctor

c) Who works in a factory?
( ) the worker
( ) the sailor
( ) the reporter

d) Who plays football?
( ) the nurse
( ) the secretary
( ) the football player

5. Complete as frases com as palavras abaixo.

> teaches – cooks – works – writes
> sings – lives

a) Mark is a sailor.
He _____ in the sea.

b) Anne is a cook.
She _____ very well.

c) Betty is a teacher.
She _____ English.

d) John is a worker.
He _____ in a big factory.

e) Donald is a farmer.
He _____ on the farm.

f) She is a singer.
She _____ very well.

g) Julie is a reporter.
She _____ texts for a newspaper.

6. Leia o texto e traduza-o abaixo.

I **wake up** every day at six o'clock, **wash** my face, **have** breakfast, **brush** my teeth, **take** my books and copybooks and **go** to school.

Traduza o texto acima.

7. Reescreva o texto anterior na 3ª pessoa do singular, observando as mudanças do verbo e dos pronomes possessivos (**his** no item a e **her** no item b).

a) John **wakes up** every day at six o'clock, **washes his** face,

b) Mary **wakes up** every day at six o'clock,

8. Ligue o texto às figuras:

getting up

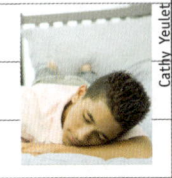

sleeping

alarm-clock ringing

having breakfast

getting on the bus

taking a shower

getting dressed

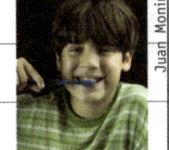

brushing the teeth

washing the face

singing a song

greeting somebody

dancing

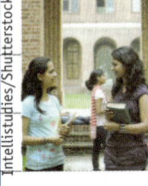

9. Observe as figuras e responda às questões a seguir.

Bob and Jim

Mr Johnson

Fred

Betty

Morgan

Lila

Robert

Rose

Mr Bronson

Jules

a) Who is playing football?

b) What is Mr Johnson doing?

c) Is Fred sleeping?

d) What is Betty doing?

e) Who is driving a car?

f) What's Rose doing?

g) Who is painting a wall?

h) Who is brushing his hair?

i) Is Mr Bronson watching TV?

j) Who is taking a shower?

Lesson 13 – Future with going to

FUTURO COM GOING TO

Bob and Jane **are going to cross** the street.

(Bob e Jane vão atravessar a rua.)

PRESENTE CONTÍNUO

Now they **are crossing** the street.

(Agora eles estão atravessando a rua.)

FUTURE

Going to é uma das várias formas de expressar o futuro e geralmente demonstra a intenção de planejamento.

Usamos o **going to** desta forma:

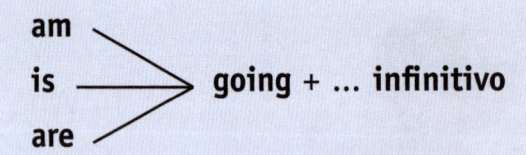

am
is ⟶ going + ... infinitivo
are

Verb to cross

I am going to cross
(Eu vou atravessar)
You are going to cross
(Você vai atravessar)
He is going to cross
(Ele vai atravessar)
She is going to cross
(Ela vai atravessar)

It is going to cross
(Ele, ela vai atravessar)
We are going to cross
(Nós vamos atravessar)
You are going to cross
(Vocês vão atravessar)
They are going to cross
(Eles, elas vão atravessar)

1. Observe o exemplo e responda às perguntas.

I am going to fish. And you?
(to play football)
I am going to play football.

a) I am going to paint a house. And you?
(to plant a tree)

b) We are going to play tennis. And they?
(to play football)

2. Responda às perguntas. Observe o exemplo.

What are you going to eat?
(a banana)
I am going to eat a banana.

a) What are you going to eat?
(an apple)

b) What is she going to eat?
(an egg)

c) What is Mary going to drink?
(milk)

d) What is Jane going to drink?
(orange juice)

e) What are the pupils going to write? (an exercise)

f) What is Flavia going to write?
(her name)

g) What is your mother going to clean? (the house)

h) What is your father going to read?
(a newspaper)

i) What are the boys going to play? (basketball)

j) I _____ going to pay the bill.
k) _____ are going to brush your teeth.
l) _____ is going to eat an apple.

3. Complete as frases com **I, you, she** ou com as formas verbais **am, is, are**.

a) You _____ going to play volleyball.

b) She _____ going to dance.

c) _____ are going to read a magazine.

d) _____ am going to write a composition.

e) I _____ going to eat a sandwich.

f) The pupils _____ going to study History.

g) The girl _____ going to take the bus.

h) She _____ going to play with you.

i) _____ is going to help you.

4. Siga os traços, descubra o que cada um dos personagens abaixo vai ler e assinale a alternativa correta.

a) Who is going to read the book?
( ) The boy
( ) The girl
( ) The man

b) Who is going to read the magazine?
( ) The boy
( ) The girl
( ) The man

c) Who is going to read the newspaper?
( ) The boy
( ) The girl
( ) The man

5. Ordene as palavras formando frases que estejam de acordo com as figuras.

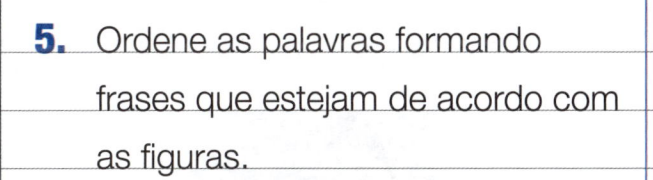

a) to play / boy / the / football / going / is

b) going / close / to / door / is / Mary / the

c) to cross / going / is / the / Paul / street

6. Ligue o animal ao seu alimento preferido (**favourite food**) e depois complete as frases abaixo.

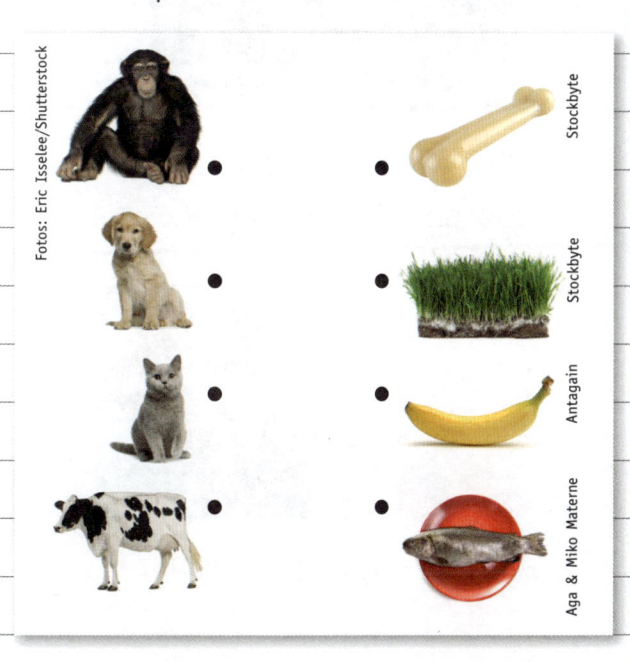

a) The monkey is going to eat

b) The dog is going

c) The cat is

d) The cow

7. Forme frases no futuro imediato ou no presente contínuo de acordo com as figuras. Veja o exemplo.

(Jane – going to watch TV)
Jane is going to watch TV.

(Now she – watching TV)
Now she is watching TV.

a) (Mary – going to swim)

(Now she – swimming)

b) (Paul – going to play football)

(Now he – playing football)

c) (Meg – going to read a letter)

(Now she – reading the letter)

d) (They – to call somebody)

(Now they – call somebody)

8. Escreva as palavras na ordem correta formando frases.

a) to give – present – are going
a – We – teacher – to – the

b) eating – cake – the – are
now – They

c) snacks – to bring – going
are – We

d) going – bring – Who – is – glasses
the – to – ?

9. Escreva as frases no futuro usando **going to**. Observe o exemplo.

Mary – to buy a magazine.
Mary is going to buy a magazine.

a) They – to drink beer.

b) I – to paint a picture.

c) We – to cross the street.

d) Jim and Sam – to eat some sweets.

e) You and I – to listen to the radio.

f) Chris – to visit a friend.

g) Liz and Lucy – to clean their bedrooms.

c) (is going to bring some snacks – a cake)

10. Observe o exemplo. Escreva os diálogos.

(going to give a watch to the teacher – a book)
– Are you going to give a watch to the teacher?
– No, I'm going to give a book.

a) (going to celebrate the Independence Day – Teacher's Day)

b) (going to decorate the bedroom – the living room)

CURIOSITIES
THE ORIGIN OF THE TRAFFIC LIGHTS

Garret Augustus Morgan (1877-1963).

In 1923 he patented a version of the traffic lights.

He sold the rights of his invention to the General Eletric Company for $ 40.000 dollars.

Morgan assistiu a um desastre de um carro e uma carruagem num cuzamento. Daí surgiu a ideia de inventar sinais para facilitar o trânsito de carros, carruagens e pedestres.

WORD BANK
traffic lights: farol
sold: vendeu
rights: direitos

Dictation

11. Ouça com atenção o ditado que o professor vai apresentar e escreva.

ANOTAÇÕES

Lesson 14 – Interrogative words - I

WHO IS THE MAN?

He is from Germany.
He is a famous scientist.
He was born in Germany on March 14, 1879.
His hair is white in this photo.
His name is Albert Einstein.
He died on April 18, 1955.

PALAVRAS E EXPRESSÕES INTERROGATIVAS

Who (quem)
   Who are you? (Quem é você?)
What (qual, o que)
   What's your name? (Qual é seu nome?)
   What's this? (O que é isto?)
Where (onde, de onde)
   Where are you from? (De onde você é?)

When (quando)
   When was he born?
   (Quando ele nasceu?)
How old (que idade, quantos anos)
   How old are you? (Qual a sua idade?)
What color (que cor)
   What color is the sky? (Que cor é o céu?)

1. Observe a fotografia e responda às perguntas, siga o exemplo das respostas que estão no boxe acima.

a) Who is the man in the picture?

b) What is his name?

c) Where is he from?

d) When was he born?

e) How old was he when he died?

f) What color is his hair in the photo?

2. Escreva a pergunta apropriada à resposta. Observe o exemplo.

– How old are you?
– I am twenty-five years old.

a) –
– My name is Flavia.

b) –
– I am from Salvador.

c) –
– My book is on the table.

d) –
– She was born in Fortaleza.

e) –
– I was born in 1995.

3. Observe o exemplo e responda às perguntas.

– How old is the teacher?
(thirty-seven)
– **The teacher is thirty-seven.**

a) – How old are you? (sixteen)

b) – How old is your city?
(one hundred years old)

c) – How old is that monument?
(fifty years old)

4. Observe o modelo e responda às perguntas.

– What's your dog's name? (Nero)
– **It's Nero.**

a) – What's your cat's name? (Billy)

b) – What's the name of your doll? (Baby)

c) – What's his name? (Robert)

d) – What's her name? (Monique)

e) – What's your name? (Henry)

f) – What's the name of your country? (Brazil)

c) – Where are you from? (Brazil)

d) – Where is Schumacker from? (Germany)

5. Complete as frases com a palavra ou expressão interrogativa adequada.

a) – _____ is your name?
   My name is Francis.

e) – Where is president Dilma Rousseff from? (Minas Gerais)

b) – _____ are you?
   I am sixty years old.

7. Complete as perguntas e a cruzadinha a seguir com as palavras que estão faltando nos diálogos.

c) – _____ are you from?
   – I am from Ceará.

6. Observe o exemplo e responda às perguntas.

1. – _____ are you from?
   – I am from Recife.
2. – _____ is your mother?
   – She is forty-four years old.

– Where are you from? (France)
– I am from France.

3. – What is _____ name?
   – My name is Silvia.

a) – Where is Margareth from? (Canada)

4. – _____ is your name?
   – My name is Ronald.
5. – Where are you _____?
   – I am from Goiânia.

b) – Where is that boy from? (Caxias)

6. – What is your _____?
   – My name is Rony Steinberg.
7. – _____ are you?
   – I'm 1.6 m tall.

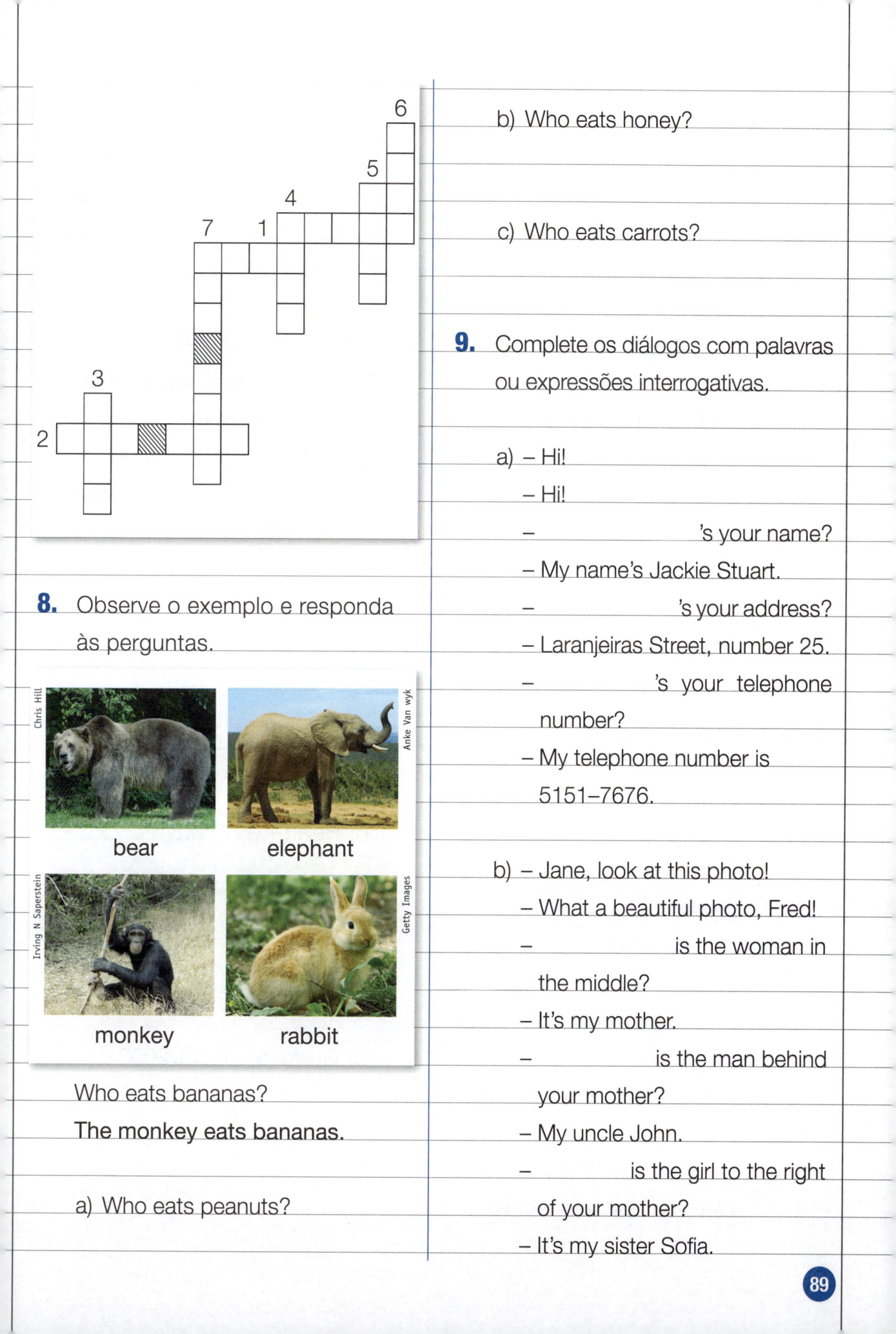

8. Observe o exemplo e responda às perguntas.

bear   elephant
monkey rabbit

Who eats bananas?
The monkey eats bananas.

a) Who eats peanuts?

b) Who eats honey?

c) Who eats carrots?

9. Complete os diálogos com palavras ou expressões interrogativas.

a) – Hi!
– Hi!
– _____ 's your name?
– My name's Jackie Stuart.
– _____ 's your address?
– Laranjeiras Street, number 25.
– _____ 's your telephone number?
– My telephone number is 5151–7676.

b) – Jane, look at this photo!
– What a beautiful photo, Fred!
– _____ is the woman in the middle?
– It's my mother.
– _____ is the man behind your mother?
– My uncle John.
– _____ is the girl to the right of your mother?
– It's my sister Sofia.

– Oh, she's very pretty.
– _____ is the boy to the right of your mother?
– It's my friend Jack.
– _____ is the girl wearing a red dress in front of you?
– It's my cousin Brenda.

c) O professor quer saber a origem dos alunos, de seus pais, avós, e começa perguntando:

– Marcos, _____ are you from?
– I'm from Porto Alegre, in Rio Grande do Sul.

– And your grandparents, _____ were they from?
– They were from Italy.

– Now you, Silvia. _____ are you from?
– I am from Rio.

– And your parents, _____ are they from?
– They are from Minas.

– _____ is from Bahia?
– I am from Salvador, Bahia.

10. Observe o exemplo e escreva os diálogos entre o professor, e os alunos, ele quer saber dos alunos a data de aniversário de cada um deles.

Marcos – 26/9/1995
Teacher: Marcos, when were you born?
Marcos: I was born on the twenty-sixth of September nineteen ninety-five.

a) Juliana: 16/4/1997

b) Helen – 9/7/1998

c) Gustavo – 10/11/2000

11. Há outra maneira de perguntar sobre a data de aniversário. Observe o exemplo abaixo e escreva os diálogos.

Marcos – 26/9
– Marcos, when is your birthday?
– My birthday is on the twenty-sixth of September.

a) Juliana – 16/4

b) Chris – 7/10

c) Alice – 2/5

12. Crie pequenos diálogos empregando palavras ou expressões interrogativas.

a)

b)

c)

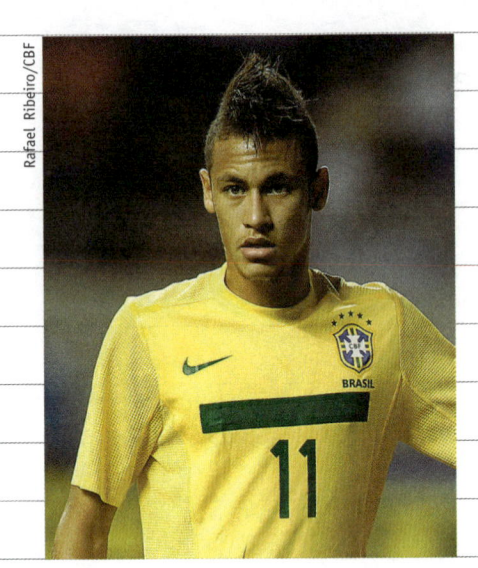

13. Observe a fotografia e responda às perguntas utilizando as respostas que estão no boxe 1 ao lado.

a) Who is the young man in the picture?

b) What is his occupation?

c) Where is he from?

d) Is he young or old?

e) When was he born?

f) How old is he now?

g) What color is his hair?

h) Where is he playing football?

Boxe 1
He is young.
His hair is black.
His name is Neymar.
He was born in 1992.
He is from Mogi das Cruzes, Brazil.
He is playing football in ...
He is a famous football player.

Observação:

Colour: cor (inglês britânico)
Color: cor (inglês americano)

Lesson 15 – Interrogative words - II

- Hi Jane! **How old** are you?
- I'm sixteen years old.
- **How tall** are you?
- I'm one meter and seventy.
- **How heavy** are you?
- I'm sixty-five kilos.

- **How** was your exam, John?
- I think I did OK, Mom.
- **What's** the new teacher **like**?
- She is kind and very attentive.
- **What's** your teacher's name?
- My teacher's name is Lyla.

PALAVRAS E EXPRESSÕES INTERROGATIVAS

a) **How**

How are you? (Como vai você?)
How tall are you?
(Que altura você tem?) para (pessoas)
How high is the mountain?
(Que altura tem a montanha?)
(edifícios, montanhas, árvores...)
How heavy are you?
(Qual é seu peso?)
How much: quanto
How much is the magazine?
(Quanto custa a revista?)

How many states are there in Brazil?
How many: quantos, quantas.
(Quantos estados há no Brazil?)

b) **What**

What's she **like**? (Como ela é?)
What... like?
Pergunta usada para se obter uma opinião ou descrição de pessoas ou coisas.
- **What**'s she **like**? (Como ela é?)
  She is tall, thin, beautiful and intelligent.
  (Ela é alta, magra, bonita e inteligente.)

1. Traduza os dois diálogos da abertura.

a)

b)

2. Complete o diálogo abaixo com palavras ou expressões interrogativas.

– _____ is Helen?
– She's fine.
– _____ is her boyfriend?
– He's fine.
– _____ 's he _____?
– He's short and thin.
– _____ are his eyes?
– His eyes are blue.
– _____ is his name?
– His name is Roy.

3. Observe o exemplo e escreva os diálogos.

Mary / well
– How is Mary?
– Mary is well.

a) your mother / well

b) your father / all right

c) the teacher / sick

d) your girlfriend / fine

e) you / fine

f) John / not well

4. Observe o exemplo, escreva em inglês e traduza os diálogos.

dad / tall
– What's your dad like?
– Como é seu pai?
– He is tall.
– Ele é alto.

a) mom / beautiful

b) girlfriend / very pretty

c) teacher (he) / strict

d) your friend / fat and short

e) Jane / kind

5. Observe o exemplo e encontre (no boxe 2) a tradução e perguntas adequadas ao diálogo.

Boxe 2
(Traduções para português)
No açougue
Na padaria
No consultório médico
No consultório do dentista
Na banca de jornais

(Perguntas em inglês)
How much is this cake?
How much is this magazine?
How much is the appointment?
How much are these sausages?
How much is to draw out a tooth?

At the grocer's (Na mercearia)

– How much are these apples?

– Fifty cents each one.

At the butcher's

(   )

–

– Five dollars per kilogram.

At the newsstand

(   )

–

– It's four dollars.

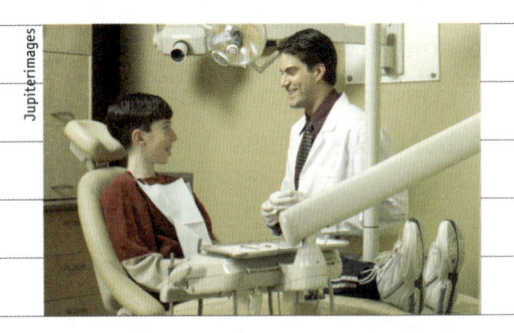

At the bakery's

(   )

–

– It's nine dollars.

At the dentist's

(   )

–

– It's twenty dollars.

At the doctor's

(   )

–

– It's ninety dollars.

6. Observe o exemplo e responda às perguntas sobre a altura das pessoas.

How tall is the teacher? (1,75)
The teacher is one meter and seventy-five centimeters tall.

a) – How tall is your mother? (1,64)

b) – How tall is your father? (1,70)

c) – How tall is Bob, the basketplayer? (1,96)

d) – How tall are you?
 I am

e) – Are you tall or short?
 I am

7. Observe o exemplo e responda às perguntas sobre o peso de pessoas ou coisas.

– How heavy is your mother? (67)
– My mother is sixty-seven kilograms heavy.

a) – How heavy is the baby? (5)

b) – How heavy is this watermelon? (14)

c) – How heavy is this elephant? (1.500)

d) – How heavy are you?
   I am...

e) – Are you heavy or light?
   I am

8. Responda às questões, utilizando dos dados entre parênteses. Observe o exemplo.

– How high is the peak of Neblina? (3.014 meters high / in Brazil)
– **The peak of Neblina is 3.014 meters high. It is in Brazil.**

a) – How high is the Eiffel Tower? (300 meters / in Paris)

b) – How high are the Petronas Towers? (452 meters / in Malaysia):

c) – How high is peak of Everest? (8.848 meters / in Himalaia)

d) – How high is the statue of Cristo Redentor? (38 meters / in Rio de Janeiro)

9. Observe as figuras e responda às questões da tabela abaixo.

WHAT IS SHE LIKE? / WHAT IS HE LIKE?

Ann / 20 years
60 kg – 1,60 m

Paul / 18 years
80 kg – 1,70 m

Rose / 14 years
45 kg – 1,55 m

John / 60 years
80 kg – 1,60 m

About Ann	What's her name? _____ How tall is she? _____ How old is she? _____ How heavy is she? _____ What's she like? Her hair is _____
About Paul	What's his name? _____ How tall is he? _____ How old is he? _____ How heavy is he? _____ What is he like? (hair and eyes): _____
About Rose	What's her name? _____ How tall is Rose? _____ How old is she? _____ How heavy is she? _____ What's Rose like? (hair and eyes): _____
About John	What's his name? _____ How tall is John? _____ How old is he? _____ How heavy is he? _____ What's John like? (hair and eyes): _____

Lesson 16 – Possessive adjectives

Mary is shopping with **her** mother and **her** brother.

Bruno is walking with **his** dog. **Its** name is Toby.

POSSESSIVE ADJECTIVES (ADJETIVOS POSSESSIVOS)

Personal pronouns — **Possessive adjectives**

I → My → meu(s), minha(s)
You → Your → seu(s), sua(s), teu(s), tua(s)
He → His → dele, seu(s), sua(s)
She → Her → dela, seu(s), sua(s)
It → Its → dele, dela, seu(s), sua(s)
We → Our → nosso(s), nossa(s)
You → Your → seu(s), sua(s)
They → Their → deles, delas, seu(s), sua(s)

Observação:

O possessivo **his** refere-se a um possuidor que é sempre uma pessoa do sexo masculino, exemplo:

Bruno is walking with **his** dog.
(Bruno está caminhando com seu cachorro.)

O possessivo **her** refere-se a um possuidor que é sempre uma pessoa do sexo feminino, exemplo:

Mary is shopping with **her** mother and **her** brother.
(Mary está fazendo compras com sua mãe e seu irmão.)

1. Complete as frases de modo que o possuidor seja do sexo feminino.

a) Paul and his father are shopping. Mary and _____ father are shopping.

b) Bruno is shopping with his brother. Mary is shopping with _____ brother.

c) John is with his sister. Rose is with _____ sister.

d) Paul is shopping with his friend. Betty is walking with _____ friend.

e) Bruno is walking with his dog Toby. Anna is walking with _____ dog Chuby.

2. Observe o exemplo e faça os exercícios.

(I) **My** socks are white.
(We) **Our** socks are white.
(He) **His** car is old.
(She) **Her** mother is very nice.
(You) **Your** books are here.
(They) **Their** shoes are expensive.

a) (I) _____ dog is big.

b) (You) _____ dog is beautiful.

c) (He) _____ mother is shopping.

d) (She) _____ father is young.

e) (We) _____ teachers are nice.

f) (They) _____ parents work in a hospital.

3. Passe para o plural. Observe o exemplo.

Her blouse is white.
Their blouses are white.

a) His car is blue.

b) His house is modern.

c) My pencil is black.

d) Your bike is blue.

4. Observe o exemplo e faça os exercícios.

This pencil belongs to me.
It's my pencil.

a) This book belongs to you.

b) This book belongs to John.

c) That doll belongs to Mary.

d) This purse belongs to Margaret.

e) This ball belongs to me.

f) Those houses belong to my parents.

5. Complete as lacunas das perguntas de acordo com o pronome pessoal das respostas:

a) What is _____ occupation?
   I am a teacher.
b) What is _____ occupation?
   He is a driver.

c) What are _____ occupations?
   They are football players.

ANOTAÇÕES

Lesson 17 – Possessive case

- Excuse me, where is **Betty's house**?
- **Betty's house** is the last house of this street.
- Is it on the left or on the right?
- It is on the right.
- Thank you.

CASO POSSESSIVO OU CASO GENITIVO

Quando o possuidor de algo é pessoa, o caso possessivo consiste geralmente no esquema: possuidor + 's + coisa possuída. Observe:

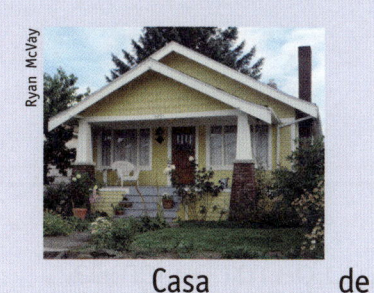

Casa	de	Betty	Betty's	house
possuidor				coisa possuída

1. Traduza o diálogo acima.

Observações:

No entanto, se o possuidor não for pessoa, o caso possessivo em inglês segue o mesmo esquema do português:

The leg **of** the table.
(Perna da mesa.)

2. Observe o exemplo e escreva da forma correta.

Boneca de Maria.
Mary's doll.

a) Carro do Paul.

b) Bola do Peter.

c) Cachorro do Robert.

d) Livro da Sílvia.

e) Casa do Albert.

f) Caneta da Mary.

a) A revista da mulher.
(magazine / the woman)

b) A bicicleta do menino.
(bicycle / the boy)

c) O caderno do aluno.
(copybook / the pupil)

d) O amigo da minha família.
(friend / my family)

3. Observe o exemplo e forme frases, usando o caso possessivo.

O carro do homem. (car / the man)
The man's car.

Observações:

Se o possuidor for nome de pessoa que termine por **s**, pode-se colocar apenas apóstrofo ou, então, apóstrofo seguido de **s**.

4. Observe o exemplo e escreva usando o caso genitivo.

Carro do Charles. (car / Charles)
Charles' car ou **Charles's car.**

a) Boneca da Doris. (doll / Doris)

b) Fazenda do Louis. (farm / Louis)

c) Mãe do Denis. (mother / Denis)

> **Observações:**
> Quando o possuidor estiver no plural e terminar com **s**, usa-se apenas apóstrofo.

5. Observe o exemplo e escreva usando o possessivo caso.

Os livros dos alunos.
(books / the students)
The students' books.

a) Os carros dos professores.
   (cars / the teachers)

b) A bola dos meninos.
   (ball / the boys)

c) Os livros das meninas.
   (books / the girls)

d) O amigo de meus pais.
   (friend / my parents)

6. Construa frases usando o caso possessivo. Observe o exemplo.

This / family / John
This is John's family.

house / Mary / red
Mary's house is red.

a) That / car / Joseph

b) This / dress / Mary

c) dog / John / black

d) ball / Jack / yellow

e) house / Mary / beautiful

f) book / Ronald / difficult

g) pens / Jane / blue

h) shoes / Mark / black

Observações:

Não se usa (**'s**) ou (**'**) com relação a coisas. Observe:

The legs **of the** table.

(As pernas da mesa.)

7. Observe o exemplo e construa as frases usando o caso possessivo.

As pernas da cadeira. (legs / chair)
The legs of the chair.

a) A janela do carro.
   (window / car)

b) As cadeiras da escola.
   (chairs / school)

c) O bico do pássaro.
   (beak / bird)

d) O galho da árvore.
   (branch / tree)

8. No espaço abaixo, invente nomes de lojas, empregando o caso possessivo. Observe os exemplos.

JOHN'S MAGAZINE

THE WORKER'S SHOP

Observações:

O **'s** do caso genitivo é usado para indicar: casa de, loja de, escritório de, consultório de etc.
Veja:
– Where's Mary?
– She's at **John's** (house).

9. Responda às perguntas, usando os dados entre parênteses.

a) Where are you going?
   (to the barber's).

b) Where is she going?
   (to the butcher's).

c) Where are the boys?
   (at Ronald's).

d) Where is your mother?
   (at the doctor's).

e) Where are they going?
   (to the baker's).

f) Where are you going?
   (to the dentist's).

10. Responda às perguntas.

a) What's your teacher's name?

b) What's your father's name?

c) What's your mother's name?

d) What's our president's name?

11. Observe o uso de **whose** e traduza o diálogo entre Doris e Jane.
whose: de quem

Whose clock is this? It's Peter's.

Doris: Whose skirt is this?
Jane: It's Mary's.
Doris: And this green one? Whose is it?
Jane: It's Helen's.
Doris: Whose shirt is that? Is it Paul's?
Jane: Yes, it is.

Dictation

12. Ouça com atenção o ditado que o professor vai apresentar e escreva.

ANOTAÇÕES

Lesson 18 – Do, does.

– Hi, Mary. **Do** you work here?
– Yes, I work. (Yes, I do.)
– **Does** your brother work here, too?
– Yes, he works here with me.
  (Yes, he does. He works here with me.)

FORMA INTERROGATIVA

Emprego das formas auxiliares **do** e **does**.
Sempre que fizermos perguntas no **simple present tense** (presente simples) com verbos não auxiliares, usaremos **do** ou **does**:
Do para **I, you, we, they.**
Does para **he, she, it.**
Observe a conjugação do verbo trabalhar (**to work**), forma afirmativa e interrogativa no presente simples:

I work.	Do I work?	(Eu trabalho?)
You work.	Do you work?	(Você trabalha?)
He works.	Does he work?	(Ele trabalha?)
She works.	Does she work?	(Ela trabalha?)
It works.	Does it work?	(Ele/a trabalha?)
We work.	Do we work?	(Nós trabalhamos?)
You work.	Do you work?	(Vocês trabalham?)
They work.	Do they work?	(Eles/Elas trabalham?)

1. Traduza o texto acima.

2. Conjugue o verbo gostar (**to like**) no **simple present tense**, forma interrogativa.

Do I like?

3. Passe para a forma interrogativa. Observe o exemplo.

I study History and Geography.
Do I study History and Geography?

a) You like fruit.

b) She loves you.

c) He drinks coffee.

d) We play football or volleyball.

e) You speak English.

f) Those girls dance well.

4. Complete as frases com **do** ou **does**.

a) _____ you like ice cream?
b) _____ he love Mary?
c) _____ they go to the park?
d) _____ you have some money?
e) _____ she work on Sundays?
f) _____ they help you?
g) _____ you have a job?
h) _____ that cow give milk?
i) _____ they study at night?
j) _____ she want coffee?
k) _____ you go to the movies?
l) _____ Mr Green teach English?

5. Observe o exemplo e responda na forma interrogativa.

I like ice cream. (you)
Do you like ice cream, too?

a) John plays football. (you)

b) Monica needs money. (her brother)

c) They study in the morning. (you)

d) We watch television at night. (they)

e) I get up at seven. (they)

6. Passe para forma interrogativa e plural. Observe o exemplo.

Do I go to the park?
Do we go to the park?

a) Do you like tea?

b) Does she know me?

c) Does it run fast?

d) Does the student understand the lesson?

e) Do I go to school by bus?

f) Does she work here?

g) Does he read newspapers?

h) Do you write letters?

7. Ordene as palavras formando frases interrogativas. Observe o exemplo.

shop / you / do / that / work / in
Do you work in that shop?

a) apples / she / does / like

b) love / Flavia / you / does

c) Mr Bergson / know / you / do

8. Traduza as frases para o inglês usando as palavras entre parênteses.

Você fala inglês?
(you / speak / English)
Do you speak English?

a) Seu amigo precisa de dinheiro?
(your / friend / need / money)

b) Ela tem um carro antigo?
(she / have / an / car / old)

c) Eles estudam à noite?
(they / study / at / night)

d) Você me entende?
   (you / me / understand)

e) Você tem um bom emprego?
   (you / have / a / good / job)

f) Sua irmã ajuda você?
   (your / sister / help / you)

g) Seu pai trabalha aos domingos?
   (your / father / work /
   on / Sundays)

h) Elas conhecem a Inglaterra?
   (they / know / England)

> **Observação:**
>
> Na **short answer**, as formas verbais **do** e **does** têm o mesmo sentido do verbo da pergunta.
>
> – Do you like fruit?
> (Você gosta de fruta?)
>
> – **Yes, I do.**
> (Sim, eu gosto.)
>
> – Does she like fruit?
> (Ela gosta de fruta?)
>
> – **Yes, she does.**
> (Sim, ela gosta.)

9. Observe os exemplos e escreva as respostas.

Do you like fruit?
(Você gosta de fruta?)
Yes, I do. (Sim, eu gosto.)

Does she like fruit?
(Ela gosta de fruta?)
Yes, she does. (Sim, ela gosta.)

a) Do you get up early?
   (Você levanta cedo?)

b) Does she like you?
   (Ela gosta de você?)

c) Do they want coffee?
   (Eles querem café?)

d) Do you speak English?
   (Você fala inglês?)

e) Does your mother
   read magazines?
   (Sua mãe lê revistas?)

Lesson 19 – Do not, does not

– Do you make your bed?
– No, I **don't**.
– Does your sister make her bed?
– No, she **doesn't**.
– Who makes the beds in your house?
– My mother.

EMPREGO DAS FORMAS AUXILIARES **DO NOT** (**DON'T**) E **DOES NOT** (**DOESN'T**)

A forma negativa no **simple present tense** (presente simples) com verbos não auxiliares se faz mediante o emprego de **do not** (**don't**) ou **does not** (**doesn't**).

Do not (**don't**) para **I**, **you**, **we**, **they**.

Does not (**doesn't**) para **he**, **she**, **it**.

As formas abreviadas **don't** e **doesn't** são usadas na conversação.

Observe a conjugação do verbo fazer (**to make**), forma negativa, no **simple present tense**:

I do not make.   I don't make. (Eu não faço.)

You do not make.   You don't make. (Você não faz.)

He does not make.   He doesn't make. (Ele não faz.)

She does not make.   She doesn't make. (Ela não faz.)

We do not make.   We don't make. (Nós não fazemos.)

You do not make.   You don't make. (Vocês não fazem.)

They do not make.   They don't make. (Eles não fazem.)

1. Complete a tradução do diálogo de abertura.

– Você faz sua cama?
– Não, eu não faço.
– Sua irmã faz a cama dela?

2. Conjugue o verbo trabalhar (**to work**) no **simple present tense** (presente simples), forma negativa abreviada.

a) I _____ here.
(Eu não trabalho aqui.)

b) You _____ here.
(Você não trabalha aqui.)

c) He _____ here.
(Ele não trabalha aqui.)

d) We _____ here.
(Nós não trabalhamos aqui.)

e) You _____ here.
(Vocês não trabalham aqui.)

f) They _____ here.
(Eles não trabalham aqui.)

3. Conjugue o mesmo verbo na forma negativa não abreviada.

4. Qual das duas formas negativas é usada na conversação: a forma abreviada ou a forma por extenso?

5. Complete as frases com **don't** ou **doesn't**.

a) I _____ understand.
b) She _____ work here.
c) They _____ play tennis.
d) I _____ know that man.
e) He _____ love me.
f) Karen _____ eat meat.
g) She _____ tell lies.
h) It _____ rain often here.
i) John _____ like coffee.
j) I _____ have any money.
k) The students _____ study.
l) We _____ work on weekends.

Lembre que:
Nas formas negativa e interrogativa o verbo principal tem a forma do infinitivo sem **to**:
to tell – contar

Affirmative
She **tells** lies. (Ela conta mentiras.)

Negative
She does not **tell** lies. (Ela não conta mentiras.)

6. Escreva na forma negativa não abreviada. Observe os exemplos.

I understand you.
I do not understand you.

He tells histories.
He does not tell histories.

a) Susan likes ice cream.

b) Mr Benson teaches English.

c) She dances well.

d) He drinks coffee.

e) I know you.

f) The shops open on Sundays.

g) We go to the movies.

h) The girls play football well.

i) I watch television in the morning.

j) I study at night.

k) She loves you.

7. Passe as frases para o inglês, utilizando das palavras entre parênteses. Observe o exemplo.

Você não precisa de dinheiro.
(you – need – money)
You don't need money.

a) Eles não estudam à noite.
   (they – study – at – night)

b) Ela não me ajuda.
   (she – help – me)

c) George não conhece você.
   (George – know – you)

d) Eu não trabalho aos domingos.
   (I – work – on – Sundays)

e) Eles não dançam bem.
   (they – dance – well)

8. Responda por extenso, na forma negativa. Observe os exemplos.

Do they want coffee?
No, they do not want coffee.
Does your sister help you?
No, my sister does not help me.

a) Does your mother like her job?

b) Do you know my father?

c) Does your sister make her bed?

9. Observe os exemplos e responda na forma negativa.

Do you like football?
(Você gosta de futebol?)
No, I don't. (Não, eu não gosto.)

Does she like coffee?
(Ela gosta de café?)
No, she doesn't. (Não, ela não gosta.)

a) Do you get up early?

b) Do you speak English?

c) Does she like you?

f) Does Monica study at night?

d) Do they work on Saturdays?

g) Do they go to the beach?

e) Does your father have a good job?

h) Do you understand me?

10. Observe o exemplo. Responda às perguntas da tabela escolhendo as expressões da tabela abaixo.

About you			
Do you eat vegetables?	Yes, I do.	No, I don't.	Sometimes I do.
Do you go to bed early?			
Do you play football?			
Do you study English?			
Do you practice sports?			
Do you go to the beach?			
Do you help your mother at home?			

11. Observe a tabela e responda às perguntas a seguir.

	to read	to swim	to eat chocolate	to drink lemonade	to sleep early
Mary	likes	doesn't like	likes	likes	doesn't like
Peter	likes	doesn't like	doesn't like	likes	likes
John	doesn't like	likes	likes	likes	doesn't like
Helen	likes	likes	doesn't like	likes	likes
Diana	doesn't like	likes	likes	doesn't like	likes
Linda	likes	likes	likes	likes	likes

a) Who likes to eat chocolate?

b) Who doesn't like to eat chocolate?

c) Who doesn't like to drink lemonade?

d) Does Peter like to sleep early?

e) Does Helen like to read?

f) Does Diana like to swim?

g) Does John like to read?

h) Who likes everything?

i) Do Linda and Diana like chocolate?

j) Do Mary and Peter like to swim?

Additional texts

PERSONAL INFORMATION

Name: Gina
Age: 12
Grade: 6th
Birthday: June 18
Country: Brazil
Interests: TV, swimming

1. Look at the identification card above and fill in your card:

Name: _____
Age: _____ Grade: _____
Birthday: _____
Country: _____
Interests: _____

2. Answer about you:

a) What is your first name?

b) What is your last name?

c) How old are you?

d) What grade are you in?

e) When is your birthday?

f) Where are you from?

g) What are your interests?

3. Read Gina's letter and complete the letter below.

Dear friend Ana
 I am Gina Martinelli. I am twelve years old. My birthday is on June 18. I am from Campinas. I am in the sixth grade at Pelegrino School. I like to study English, watch TV and swimming. I am sending you a photo of my family. I am near my father in the photo. What about you? Write me soon.
                                              Gina

Now, complete your letter to a friend.
Dear,
I am _____ . I am _____ years old. I'm from _____ .
I like to _____ and _____ , but I don't like to _____
What about you?
Write me soon. Love, from _____ .

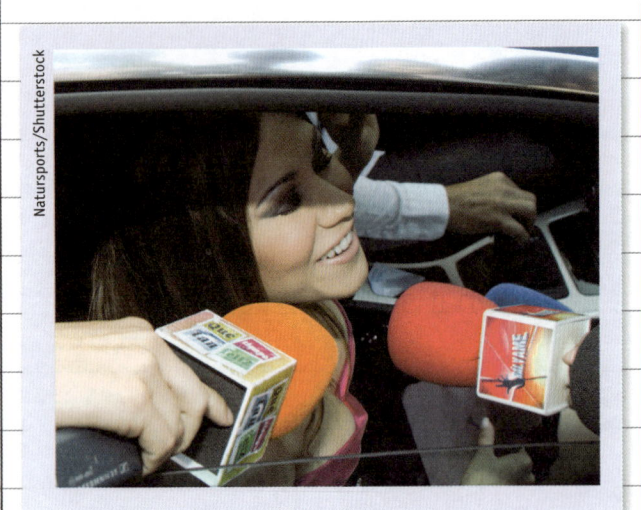

AN INTERVIEW

– Is this your first song of success?
– What's your name, please?
– How old are you?
– What are you planning for your next album?
– Where are you from?
– Thank you very much.

MARINA, A YOUNG SINGER

– I am planning to compose some songs about children, violence and the environment.
– Yes, it is.
– My name is Marina Cintra.
– I am from Brazil.
– I am twenty-five years old.
– You're welcome. It's a pleasure to talk to you.

1. Organize na ordem correta o diálogo entre o repórter e a jovem cantora.

2. Releia o texto que você organizou e responda.

a) What's the singer's name?

b) Where is she from?

c) How old is the young singer?

d) What's the TV reporter's name?

e) Is the young singer planning to compose a song about football?

f) Is she planning to compose songs about violence and the environment?

ON APRIL 1ST | APRIL FOOL'S DAY

A FESTIVAL FOR JOKES AND TRICKS

April 1st is April Fool's Day in Britain and in the United States. This is a very old tradition from the Middle Ages. At that time the servants were masters for one day, giving orders to their masters.

Now April Fool's Day is different. It's a day for jokes and tricks.

In Brazil, people often tell lies.

VOCABULARY
April Fool's Day: 1º de abril, Dia da Mentira
Middle Ages: Idade Média
masters: senhores, patrões
servants: servos, escravos
day for jokes and tricks: dia de contar piadas e pregar peças
people: pessoas
tell lies: contam mentiras

3. Ligue, de acordo com o texto:

The servants were masters — it's a day for jokes and tricks.

April Fool's Day — for one day.

On April Fool's Day — is April Fool's Day.

April 1st — people often tell lies.

4. Responda em inglês.

a) When is April Fool's Day?

b) Is April Fool's Day an old tradition in England?

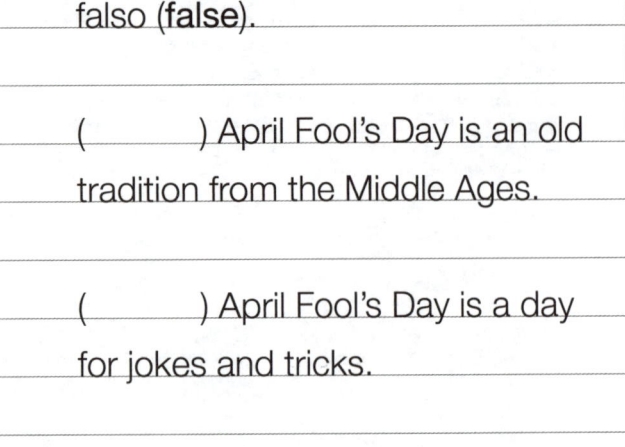

APRIL FOOL'S DAY

Bob: As you know... I have four palaces: one in England, one in Italy, one in Portugal and one in Brazil... Next month my friend, Prince of Persia, is coming to visit me in my palace in Brazil...

Jim: Prince of Persia?!! It's impossible!!

Bob: Yes, the Prince is coming to visit me...

WORD BANK
as you know: como você sabe
palaces: palácios
next month: no próximo mês
is coming to visit me: vem me visitar

5. Escreva verdadeiro (**true**) ou falso (**false**).

(   ) April Fool's Day is an old tradition from the Middle Ages.

(   ) April Fool's Day is a day for jokes and tricks.

(   ) In the Middle Ages, masters were servant for many days.

6. Responda em inglês de acordo com o texto.

a) Quem está pregando uma peça de primeiro de abril: é Jim ou é Bob?

b) Em que países Bob diz que possui palácios?

c) Quem acha impossível que o príncipe da Pérsia venha visitar o Bob?

d) Quando o príncipe da Pérsia viria visitar o Bob?

e) Em que país o príncipe da Pérsia viria visitar o Bob?
   (   ) In Italy
   (   ) In Brazil

f) Pode-se dizer que o texto combina com April Fool's Day?
   (   ) Yes   (   ) No

BEWARE OF THE SUN!

Do you like to go to the beach on a sunny day?
Do you spend much time tanning your body in the sun?
Some sunshine is good for you, but too much sun can be dangerous.
Too much sun can cause skin cancer.
Beware of the sun from 10 a.m. to 3 p.m.
At the beach, use sunscreen.

7. Write (**true**) or (**false**) according to the text.

a) Some sunshine is good. (   )
b) Too much sunshine is dangerous. (   )
c) Too much sunshine is not dangerous. (   )

8. Complete according to the text.

a) _____ like to go to the beach _____ a sunny day?
b) _____ spend _____ time tanning _____ body in the sun?
c) Sunlight is dangerous _____ 10 a.m. _____ 3 p.m.
d) _____ the beach, _____ sun screen.

9. Answer the questions.

a) Do you like to go to the beach?
   (   ) Yes, I like.
   (   ) No, I don't.
   (   ) Sometimes.

b) Do you spend much time tanning your body in the sun?
   (   ) Yes, I do.
   (   ) No, I don't.
   (   ) Sometimes I do.

c) What can too much sun cause?
   It can cause _____

HAPPY FATHER'S DAY

In Brazil, we celebrate Father's Day on the second Sunday in August.

In the United States, they celebrate Father's Day on the third Sunday in June.

FOLKLORE

What is folklore?

The word folklore comes from English and means "popular knowledge": folk = people, lore = knowledge.

Brazilian folklore is very rich. We have a mixture of Indian folklore, Portuguese folklore, African folklore and immigrant folklore.

Many countries celebrate folklore on August 22nd.

In English folklore it is good luck to see black cats. In Brazil it is bad luck to see black cats.

10. Responda de acordo com o texto.

a) When do we celebrate Father's Day in Brazil?

b) When do Americans celebrate Father's Day?

Traduza o texto.

11. Escreva em português o título do texto.

SENDING LETTERS

Ted, Bob, Anne and Mary are going to the post-office.

Ted is sending a letter to a friend in Japan, and Bob a postcard to France. Anne is sending letters to England.

12. Complete according to the text.

a) Ted, Bob, Anne and Mary _____ post-office.

b) Ted is _____ Japan.

13. Find the pairs (Relacione, de acordo com o texto).

(1) Ted   ( ) is sending a postcard to France.

(2) Bob   ( ) is sending a letter to Japan.

(3) Anne   ( ) is sending letters to England.

14. Answer.

a) What are Ted, Bob, Anne and Mary doing?

b) Is Ted sending a letter or a postcard?

c) What is Bob sending?

WHO'S THE OWNER?
Diana: Whose skirt is this?
Karen: It's Mary's.
Diana: And this green one? Is it Mary's too?
Karen: No, it is not. It's Helen's.
Diana: And this blue shirt? Is it Peter's?
Karen: Yes, it is.

15. Answer according to the text.

a) Is the green skirt Helen's?

b) Is the blue shirt Helen's?

c) Is the blue shirt Peter's?

16. Find the pairs:

(1) Whose skirt ( ) it is.
(2) Yes, ( ) it is not.
(3) No, ( ) is this?

We are washing the dog.

What are they doing?

I am drawing a different tree.

What is the boy doing?

Diana's plans for this week

Monday	Go to the dentist's.
Tuesday	Visit Mary in the evening.
Wednesday	An interview for a job.
Thursday	Write some letters.
Friday	Go shopping with my mother.
Saturday	Go to the cinema.
Sunday	Visit friends.

17. Leia a rotina de Diana e responda. Veja o modelo.

– When is Diana going to visit her friends?
– **On Sunday. (She is going to visit her friends on Sunday.)**

a) – Is she going to visit Mary on Tuesday evening?

b) – When is she going to the dentist's?

c) – When is she planning to go shopping?

He is a magician

Oh! This is multiplication of money! It is forbidden. Follow me to the police station!

Look! A magician! He is taking money from a top hat.

Oh! It's fantastic!

Secretary: What's your name, please?
Visitor: Mr Schartzwynezcky.
Secretary: What??!!
Visitor: With y at the end.
Secretary: ???!!!

18. What letter is at the end of this strange name?
It is _____.

19. How many letters are there in the visitor's name?
There are _____ letters.

20. Is the visitor's name easy to write?
( ) yes, it is.   ( ) No, it is not.

Traduza o diálogo.

Title:

Spectator 1:

Spectator 2:

Policeman:

VACATION
The end of the year is coming and your vacation time, too. It's a nice time. You can enjoy your vacation in many ways:
- You can go to many places as beaches, movies, parks...
- You can practice sports.
- You can travel with your parents.
Is really a good time! Have a nice vacation!

21. Responda de acordo com o texto:

a) What is coming?

b) Is vacation time a nice time?

c) Where can you go on your vacation?

d) What can you practice on your vacation?

22. Escreva as frases usando o pronome **he** e o verbo na terceira pessoa do singular:

You enjoy your vacation.
He enjoys his vacation.

a) You visit many places.

b) You practice many sports.

c) You travel with your parents.

ANOTAÇÕES

General vocabulary

A

a: um, uma
about: sobre, aproximadamente
above: acima de
according to: de acordo com
acrobat: acrobata
address: endereço
admirer: admirador
after: depois
again: novamente
age: idade
ago: passado, atrás
air: ar
all: tudo, todos
all right: tudo bem
alligator: crocodilo
alone: só, sozinho
aloud: em voz alta
already: já
also: também
always: sempre
am: sou, estou
among: entre (muitos)
an: um, uma
and: e
angry: zangado, irritado
animal: animal
answer: resposta; responder
any: algum, qualquer
appear: aparecer
appearance: aparência
apple: maçã
appointment: encontro, compromisso
April: abril
April Fool's Day: Dia 1º de Abril
are: são, estão
are there?: há?, existem?
aren't: não são, não estão
around: ao redor de
arrangement: arranjo
at: em, no
at home: em casa
at nine: às nove
at school: na escola
August: agosto
autumn (fall): outono
avoid: evite, evitar
away: embora
awful: horrível, terrível

B

baby: bebê
back: atrás; costas
bad: ruim
bad luck: má sorte, azar
bag: sacola, mochila, pasta, mala
bakery: padaria
ball: bola
banana: banana
barber's: barbearia

barn: estábulo
basket: cesto, cesta
basketball: basquete
bathroom: banheiro
be: ser, estar
beach: praia
beak: bico
beans: feijão
bear: urso
beautiful: bonito
because: porque
bed: cama
bedroom: quarto de dormir
beer: cerveja
before: antes
begin: começar
beginning: começo, começando
begins: começa
behind: atrás
belong: pertencer
below: debaixo, abaixo
belt: cinto
between: entre (dois)
beware: cuidado
bicycle: bicicleta
big: grande
bike: bicicleta
bill: nota, conta
bird: pássaro
birthday: aniversário
black: preto

blackboard: quadro-negro
blanks: espaços brancos
blind: cego
blond: loiro
blouse: blusa
blow: soprar
blue: azul
board: quadro
boat: barco, bote
body: corpo
bone: osso
book: livro
boring: chato, enfadonho
both: ambos
box: caixa
boy: menino, rapaz
boyfriend: namorado
brake: breque
branch: galho
Brazilian: brasileiro
bread: pão
break: quebrar
breakfast: café da manhã
bright: brilhante
brightly: com muito brilho
bring: trazer, traga
Britain: Inglaterra
broken: quebrado
broom: vassoura
brother: irmão
brown: marrom

brush: escovar; escova
bucklet: baldinho
build: construir
building: edifício
bus: ônibus
bus stop: ponto de ônibus
busy: ocupado
but: mas
butter: manteiga
butterfly: borboleta
button: botão
buy: comprar
by: por
by bus: de ônibus
bye: até logo

C

cage: gaiola
cake: bolo
call: chamar, telefonar
came: veio
camera: máquina fotográfica
can: pode, podem, posso
can't: não pode
candy: bala, doce, bombom
car: carro
car racer: piloto de corrida
cards: cartas, baralho
care: cuidado
carrot: cenoura
carry: carregar

cart: carroça; carrinho
cat: gato
catch: pegar
celebrate: comemorar, celebrar
certainly: certamente
chair: cadeira
chalk: giz
change: troco
cheap: barato
cheese: queijo
chicken: frango
child: criança
children: crianças, filhos
Chinese: chinês
choice: escolha
choose: escolher
church: igreja
cinema: cinema
city: cidade
class: classe; aula
classmate: colega de classe
clean: limpar; limpo
clerk: balconista
climb: subir
clock: relógio
close: fechar
cloth: pano
clothes: roupas
cloud: nuvem
clown: palhaço
club: clube

coffee: café
cold: frio
color (colour): cor; colorir
come: vir, venho, venha
come back: voltar
comes: vem
coming: vindo
congratulations: parabéns
connect: ligar, conectar
control: controlar
cook: cozinhar; cozinheiro
copybook: caderno
could: pôde, podia, poderia
country: país; campo
cow: vaca
cowboy: vaqueiro
crawl: rastejar
crazy: louco
cross: cruz; cruzar
crosses: cruza
cry: chorar, gritar
cup: xícara
cut: cortar
cycling: ciclismo

D

dad: pai, papai
dance: dançar; dança
dancer: dançarino
day: dia
deaf: surdo
dear: querido, querida
December: dezembro
deliver: entregar
dentist: dentista
desk: carteira; mesinha
different: diferente
difficult: difícil
diligent: aplicado
dining room: sala de jantar
dirty: sujo
discoverer: descobridor
distinction: distinção
do: fazer
do not: não
doctor: médico, doutor
does not: não
doesn't: não
dog: cachorro
doing: fazendo
doll: boneca
don't: não
donkey: burro
door: porta
dot: ponto
dot to dot: ponto a ponto
down: para baixo
downtown: centro da cidade
draw: desenhar, traçar
dress: vestido
drink: beber; bebida; aperitivo
drive: dirigir

driver: motorista
drop: deixar cair
dry: secar
dumb: mudo

E

each: cada
ear: orelha
early: cedo
Earth: Terra
easy: fácil
eat: comer
egg: ovo
eight: oito
else, what else?: o que mais?
emergency: emergência
employee: empregado
empty: vazio
end: fim, terminar
engineer: engenheiro
England: Inglaterra
enjoy: desfrutar, gozar
environment: meio ambiente
equally: igualmente
evening: noite
every: cada, todos
everyday: cada dia, todos os dias
everything: tudo
every time: sempre
everywhere: em toda parte
excuse me: desculpe-me, com licença

expensive: caro
eye: olho

F

factory: fábrica
fall: cair, cachoeira, outono
false: falso
family: família
famous: famoso
fan: fã
far: longe
farm: fazenda
farmer: fazendeiro
fashion: moda
fast: rápido
fasten: apertar
fat: gordo
father: pai
February: fevereiro
feel: sentir
few: poucos
fifth: quinto
fill in: preencher
find: encontrar
fine: ótimo; bem
finger: dedo
finish: terminar
fire: fogo
fireman: bombeiro
first: primeiro
fish: peixe; pescar

fisherman: pescador
five: cinco
flag: bandeira
flower: flor
fly: voar
flying: voador, voando
follow: seguir, siga
fool: louco, bobo
food: comida
Fool's Day: Dia da Mentira
foot: pé
football: futebol
for: para, por
forbidden: proibido
forget: esquecer
forty: quarenta
four: quatro
fourteen: quatorze
fourth: quarto
France: França
Friday: sexta-feira
friend: amigo, amiga
from: de, desde
fruit: fruta, frutas
full: cheio
fun: diversão, brincadeira

G

game: jogo
garden: jardim
gate: portão

generally: geralmente
German: alemão
Germany: Alemanha
get: chegar, conseguir
get dressed: vestir-se
get off: sair
get on: subir
get out: sair
get up: levantar
girl: garota, menina, moça
girlfriend: namorada
give: dar
glass: vidro; copo
glasses: óculos, copos
go: ir, vou, vá
go away: ir embora
go back: voltar
go shopping: ir fazer compras
goalkeeper: goleiro
goat: cabra, bode
God: Deus
goes: vai
going: indo
good: bom
good afternoon: boa-tarde
good evening: boa-noite
good luck: boa sorte
good night: boa-noite
goodbye: até logo
got: conseguido
grade: nota; grau; série

grandfather: avô
grandmother: avó
grandparents: avós
grass: grama
great: grande, ótimo
green: verde

H

hair: cabelo
half: metade
hand: mão
happy: feliz
hard: duro, arduamente
hard-working: trabalhador, trabalho duro
has: tem
has got: tem
hat: chapéu
have: ter
have lunch: almoçar
he: ele
head: cabeça
hear: escutar, ouvir
heavy: pesado
hello: alô
help: socorro; ajudar
hen: galinha
her: dela
here: aqui
hey: ei
hi: oi
hidden: escondido, oculto

hide: esconder, ocultar
high: alto
highway: rodovia
him: o, lo, ele
his: dele, seu
history(ies): história(s), conto(s), narrativa(s)
hit: bater
hold: segurar
holidays: férias
home: casa (**at home:** em casa)
homework: lição de casa
honey: mel
horse: cavalo
hospital: hospital
hot: quente
hour: hora
house: casa
how: como
how many: quantos
how much: quanto
how old are you?: quantos anos você tem?
hungry: faminto, com fome
hunt: caça, caçar
husband: marido

I

I: eu
I'm: eu sou, eu estou
I'm going: eu vou

I'm sorry: sinto muito
ice cream: sorvete
if: se
improve: melhorar
in: em
in front of: na frente de
Indian: indiano, indígena, índio
interesting: interessante
intersection: cruzamento
interview: entrevista
introducing: apresentando
invite: convidar
is: é, está
island: ilha
isn't: não é, não está
it: ele, ela, o, a, lo, la
Italy: Itália

J

January: janeiro
Japan: Japão
Japanese: japonês
job: trabalho, emprego, profissão
join: juntar, ligar
joke: brincadeira, piada
juice: suco
July: julho
jump: pular
June: junho
just: apenas, exatamente

K

keep: manter, guardar
keep off: evite
key: chave
kick: chutar
kind: bondoso, gentil
kitchen: cozinha
kite: pipa, quadrado, papagaio
know: saber, conhecer
knowledge: conhecimento

L

lady: dama, senhora
lake: lago
land: terra
large: grande, amplo
last: último
late: tarde, atrasado
later: mais tarde
law: lei
lazy: preguiçoso
leaf: folha
leave: deixar, deixo
leaves: folhas; parte; deixa
left: esquerdo, partiu, deixou
legs: pernas
lemon: limão
less: menos
let me see: deixa-me ver
let's: vamos (Let's go): vamos
letter: carta, letra

lies: mentiras
life: vida
lift: elevador; carona; levantar
light: luz; leve
like: gostar; como
lion: leão
listen: ouvir
little: pouco
live: morar, viver
living room: sala de estar
long: longo, comprido
look: olhar, olhe
look at: olhar para, olhe
look for: procurar
lose turn: perde a vez
loud: barulhento (som, voz)
love: amar; amor
luck: sorte
lucky: sortudo
lunch: almoço, lanche

M

made up: feito, produzido
magazine: revista; loja
magician: mágico
mail: correio
mailman: carteiro
make: fazer, arrumar
man: homem
manager: gerente
manner: modo, maneira

many: muitos
map: mapa
March: março
market: mercado; feira
marvelous: maravilhoso
master: mestre; patrão
match: partida, jogo
matter: matéria, assunto; problema
may: pode, podem, podemos
May: maio
me: me, mim, eu
meal: refeição
mean: significar
means: meios
meat: carne
meet: encontrar (pessoas)
men: homens
mess: bagunça; desordem
middle: meio
Middle Ages: Idade Média
milk: leite
mine: meu, minha
missing: que falta
mixture: mistura
Monday: segunda-feira
money: dinheiro
monkey: macaco
month: mês
moon: lua
more: mais
morning: manhã

most: mais
mother: mãe
mount: monte
mouse: rato
moustache: bigode
mouth: boca
move: mudar
movies: cinema
much: muito
mom: mãe, mamãe
musicians: músicos
must: precisa, precisamos, precisam, preciso
my: meu, minha, meus, minhas

N

name: nome
nature: natureza
near: perto de
need: precisar
neck: pescoço
negro: negro
neighbor: vizinho
new: novo
news: notícia, notícias
newspaper: jornal
next: próximo, seguinte
nice: bonito, bom
night: noite
nine: nove
nineteen: dezenove

no: não
nobody: ninguém
none: ninguém; nenhum
nose: nariz
not: não
nothing: nada
nothing at all: de nada
November: novembro
now: agora
number: número
nurse: enfermeira

O

occupation: profissão, ocupação
October: outubro
odd: estranho, avulso
of: de
of course: naturalmente
office: escritório
office-boy: ajudante de escritório
often: frequentemente
old: velho
on: sobre
on the left: à esquerda
on the right: à direita
one: um, uma
only: somente, apenas
open: abrir, aberto
or: ou
orange: laranja
other: outro

our: nosso, nossa, nossos, nossas
owner: dono

P

pail: balde
paint: pintura; pintar
painter: pintor
pair: par
parents: pais
park: parque
party: festa
pass: passar
pay: pagar
pay attention: prestar atenção
peak: pico
peanut: amendoim
pear: pera
pen: caneta
pencil: lápis
people: pessoas, povo
pick up: pegar, apanhar
picture: pintura; fotografia
pig: porco
pilot: piloto
place: lugar
plan: plano; planejar
plane: avião
planning: planejando
plant: plantar
play: jogar, brincar; tocar instrumento musical

player: jogador
please: por favor
pocket: bolso
police station: delegacia
policeman: policial
politician: político
pool: poço; tanque
poor: pobre
populous: populoso
porter: carregador
postcard: cartão-postal
postman: carteiro
post-office: correio
potato: batata
practice: praticar
pretty: bonito
problem: problema
pudding: pudim
pull: puxar
pupils: alunos
puppies: filhotes de cachorro
purse: bolsa
push: empurrar
put: pôr, colocar

Q

quality: qualidade
queen: rainha
query: pergunta, questão
question: pergunta
quick: rápido

R

rabbit: coelho
racer: corredor
radio: rádio
rain: chuva, chover
reach: alcançar, conseguir
read: ler
reading: lendo; leitura
really: realmente
reason: razão, motivo, causa
recording: gravando
red: vermelho
refrigerator: geladeira
relatives: parentes
remember: lembrar-se
repair: consertar
reward: recompensa
rice: arroz
rich: rico
ride: montar, andar a cavalo
right: direito, certo
river: rio
road: estrada
rocket: foguete
room: sala, cômodo, quarto
rope: corda
rose: rosa
round: redondo
run: correr
runner: mensageiro
running: correndo

S

sad: triste
sail: navegar
sailor: marinheiro
sandwich: sanduíche
Saturday: sábado
saucer: pires (**flying saucer:** disco voador)
sausage: salsicha, linguiça
say: dizer, diga
school: escola
sea: mar
season: estação (ano)
seat: assento
seat belt: cinto de segurança
second: segundo
secret: segredo
secretary: secretária
see: ver
see you later: até mais tarde
see you tomorrow: até amanhã
sell: vender
send: enviar
September: setembro
servant: servo
seven: sete
seventh: sétimo
she: ela
shine: brilhar
ship: navio
shirt: camisa

shoe: sapato
shop: loja
shopping: mercadoria, compra
short: curto, baixo
shout: gritar
show: mostrar; espetáculo
shower: chuveiro (**take a shower:** tomar um banho de chuveiro)
shut: fechar
sick: doente
side: lado
sign: sinal
simplify: simplificar
sing: cantar
singer: cantor
singing: cantando
single file: fila única
sir: senhor
sister: irmã
sit: sentar
sit down: sentar
sitting: sentando, sentado
six: seis
sixth: sexto
sixty: sessenta
skin: pele
skirt: saia
sleep: dormir
slow: lento, vagaroso
slowly: vagarosamente
small: pequeno

smell: cheirar
smile: sorrir, sorria
smoke: fumar; fumaça
snack: lanche
snow: neve
Snow-White: Branca de Neve
so: tão, portanto, assim
so long: até logo, tchau
socks: meias
some: alguns
somebody: alguém
something: algo, alguma coisa
son: filho
song: canção
soon: logo
sorry: desculpa, perdão
sour: azedo
sow: semear, plantar; porca
snake: cobra
football: futebol
spaceship: nave
Spain: Espanha
Spanish: espanhol
spare time: tempo livre
speak: falar
speaker: aquele que fala, locutor
spend: gastar, passar, gastar
spider-man: homem-aranha
spider-web: teia de aranha
sport: esporte
spot: apontar, marcar; marca, mancha

spring: primavera
square: quadrado, praça
stand up: ficar de pé
star: estrela
start: começar
state: estado
station: estação
stay: ficar, permanecer
still: ainda, até
stone: pedra
stop: parar
straight: direto, em frente, reto
street: rua
strict: severo
strong: forte
student: estudante
study: estudar
summer: verão
sun: sol
Sunday: domingo
sunny: ensolarado
sunscreen lotion: protetor solar
sunshine: luz do sol
sure: certo, com certeza
surfboard: prancha de surfe
surprised: surpreso
sweet: doce
swim: nadar
swimming: natação
swimming pool: piscina
switch: trocar, mudar

T

table: mesa
tail: rabo
take: pegar, levar, tomar
talk: conversar
tall: alto
taxi-driver: motorista de táxi
tea: chá
teach: ensinar
teacher: professor
teaching: ensinando
team: time
teeth: dentes
telephone: telefone
tell: dizer
ten: dez
tennis: tênis
thank you: obrigado
thanks: obrigado
that: aquele, aquela, aquilo
the: o, a, os, as
their: deles, delas
there: lá
there are: há
there is: há
there was: havia, existia
there were: havia, existiam
these: estes, estas
they: eles, elas
thief: ladrão
thin: magro, fino

thing: coisa
think: pensar
third: terceiro
thirsty: com sede
thirty: trinta
this: este, esta
those: aqueles, aquelas
thousand: mil
three: três
throw: arremessar, lançar
Thursday: quinta-feira
ticket: bilhete, tíquete
tidy: arrumado
tiger: tigre
time: tempo, hora
tired: cansado
to: para, a
toast: torrar, tostar, torrada
today: hoje
tomato: tomate
tools: ferramentas
tortoise (turtle): tartaruga
tower: torre
town: cidade
traffic: trânsito
traffic laws: leis de trânsito
trick: travessura; trapaça; truque
twin: gêmeo

U

ugly: feio

unknown: desconhecido (a)
United Kingdom: Reino Unido
useful: útil
usually: geralmente

V

value: valor
vegetables: legumes
very: muito

W

wait: esperar
waiter: garçom
wake up: acordar, levantar
wallet: carteira
want: querer
was burn: nasceu
wash: lavar
water: água
watch: observar, vigiar
watching TV: assistindo TV
watermelon: melancia
way: caminho, maneira
weak: fraco
weather: tempo
week: semana
welcome: bem-vinda(o)
what color? De que cor?
whose: de quem
wide: amplo, vasto
wife: esposa

wish: desejo, desejar
with: com
with me: comigo
wonderful: maravilhoso
wrench: chave inglesa, chave de grifo
writer: escritor
wrong: errado

Y

year: ano
yesterday: ontem
young: jovem
younglet: filhote
you're welcome: de nada

Z

ZIP Code: Código de Endereçamento Postal (CEP)
zodiac: zodíaco, astrologia
zoo: zoológico
zucchini: abobrinha